RAMAYAN KATHA

A Simplify English Version with Lessons for Life

Sumintra Paltoo-Maharaj

Preface

Amba Devi & Sita Vani Maharaj

This book is written in loving reverence to the lotus-like feet of Sri Rama and Maata Sita based on intuition shortly after migrating to the blessed soil of the United Arab Emirates. Maata Sita and Sri Rama has always been, and will always be, my inspiration in life.

The narrative adopts a non-academic tone that is set in simple *English Language* to provide a deeper understanding of the *Holy Ramayan* as written by the great sages Valmiki and Tulsidas, and visually replicated by film producer, Ramanand Sagar. It aims towards the younger generation in particular, regardless of race, gender, religion, culture, and other differences to create awareness of the philosophy, and to provide enlightenment.

I have truthfully and solely compiled this narration to the best of my understanding, knowledge and interpretation. It is not meant in any way to disrespect or offend anyone, yet I humbly apologize for any shortcomings on my part.

I dedicate this book to my dearly beloved daughters, *Amba Devi Maharaj & Sita Vani Maharaj*, as well as, the children of the world.

Contents

Page Number

Introduction

This narrative explores the events undertaken by the characters of the *Ramayan* in sequential order. High emphasis is placed on the philosophy therein as it relates to daily life in this age of *Kaliyug*. Relevant comparisons of the teachings of few other sacred, Hindu scriptures are intertwined to produce a comprehensive and richer discourse of the compassion and glories of the *Divine Lord* and *Universal Mother*. In addition, my personal beliefs, perspectives, opinions, life's experiences and that of loved ones, in relation to the *Katha* are also integrated to add deeper meaning and to provide knowledge, insights and enlightenment.

As I prepare to extol the divine teachings of Sri Rama, I firstly bow to *Siddhi-Vinayak Ganapati Baba* who is the embodiment of wisdom and the remover of obstacles. I prostrate before *Saraswati Maata* who is the Goddess of Learning, Knowledge and the Arts. Seeking the blessings of the *Great Lord Shiva* and *Gauri Maata*, I now surrender at the lotus-like feet of *Sri Rama* and *Maata Sita* as well as, the mighty *Hanuman Baba* as I pray to stay true to this sacred and glorious *Ramayan Katha*. Lastly, I bow to my spouse, parents, preceptors, teachers, respected elders and the *Divinity* present in all Beings as I impart *Sri Rama's Katha.*

Om Jai Ram Sri Ram Jai Sri Sita Rama!!!

Rama's Childhood & Education

In the City of Ayodhya there once lived a pious and powerful King whose name was Dashrath. He was a just and righteous Emperor, who had control over his ten senses. As such, the people of Ayodhya were contented, and they lived happily. Being a descendant of the *'Raghuvansha-Ikshvaku-Suryavansha'* Dynasty, Dasrath honored the foremost oath of his lineage that declared, *'Raghukula reeti saada chale aye, praan jaaye para vaachana na jaaye.'* It simply meant that the governing principle of the Raghukul Dynasty was to stay true to their spoken word, even at the cost of their lives. In other words, they were prepared to give up their life, but not go back on their given word. Such was the high ideals of the Raghukul lineage that carried forth the emblem of the Sun as their diety was Lord Surya, who governs the Sun.

King Dasrath had three wives - Kaushalya, Sumitra and Kaikeyi as were customary for a King. Moreover, he married again and again to beget offspring as heir to the throne. Many years had passed, and the King and his Queens were still longing for a child. One day, as King Dasrath looked into the mirror, he noticed the grey hair peeping out at the side of his ear. At that sign of aging, the King grew pale with worry as he did not have a son to succeed him and to carry forth his lineage.

The next day, barefooted leaving behind his Royal attire and army, the King proceeded independently on foot to his *Guru* (Godfather), Vashistha. As a beggar seeking alms, the King expressed his heart's desire and concerns to his Guru. Vashistha understood the burning desire of the King and thus, advised him to seek the help of Sage Rishyasringa to perform the *Putrakameshti Yagna*, a specific ritual to beget children.

When something is critically important to us, and we need the help of someone, it is essential to seek help from the most appropriate person that is both, trustworthy and reliable to effectively guide us towards achieving our desires and goals. Moreover, regardless of our socioeconomic or political status, it is vitally important that we approach our potential adviser/helper with humility and sincerity to communicate and achieve our purpose. In that way, the person we approach seeking help or favor may feel inclined to help us.

As advised by the Sage, the King performed the *Yagna* (sacrifice) to the chanting of mystic mantras, while offering oblations into the sacred fire. Pleased with the devotion of the King, the deity of fire, *Agni Devata* emerged from the sacred fire with a bowl of *kheer* (rice pudding) which he gladly presented to King Dasrath. Agni Devata advised the King to distribute the holy offerings among his three Queens. Ecstatically, the King returned home and presented the small bowl of nectar to his Queens. The *kheer* was divided into half, between Kaushalya and Kaikeyi, of which both Queens gave one half of their share to Queen Sumitra.

Consequently, all three queens conceived and in due course of time, in the month of *Chaitra* (March-April) at the midday hour, when it was neither hot nor cold, and a cool, sweet fragrant breeze filled the atmosphere, the Lord manifested on Earth as Queen Kaushalya's baby. Simultaneously, Kaikeyi and Sumitra begot baby boys as well. Kaushalya's son was named *Ram/Rama*, and Kaikeyi's son was named *Bharat*, while Sumitra had twins and her sons were named *Lakshman* and *Shatrughna*.

Unknowingly to anyone, the babies were Divine incarnations. That meant, Rama was the incarnation of the Lord of the Universe, *Maha Vishnu*, while Bharat and Shatrughna were sparks of that same Divinity. On the other hand, Lakshman was the incarnation of *Sheesnag*, the King Serpent that Maha Vishnu and his beautiful consort, Maha Lakshmi rest on in the milky ocean in *Vaikuntha*.

The boon of having the Divine Lord manifested in their home was conferred upon King Dasrath and Queen Kaushalya in their prior birth as *Manu* and *Satrupa*. They had performed intense austerity to have the Lord of the Universe incarnate in their home as their son. Moreover, people were at that time faced with ongoing atrocities and sufferings by the demon King, Ravan.

Hence, Mother Earth adopted the form of a cow and approached the *Sustainer of the Universe*, Maha Vishnu for his help to restore peace and happiness on Earth. The merciful Lord assured Mother Earth of his help, and at the opportune time, He manifested in the home of Dasrath and Kaushalya. Thus, the King and his Queens, as well as the people of Ayodhya rejoiced in ecstasy at the birth of the four babies.

In another beautiful City known as Mithila or Janakpur, there lived another most pious and righteous King by the name of Janak who was an ardent devotee of Lord Shiva. Mithila was faced with severe drought and famine. Thus, one day as the fields were being plowed, the plow got stuck on a box buried in the soil. Upon opening the box, to the surprise of the King and his subjects, a most beautiful baby girl was found inside the box. She was named, Sita who in reality was the incarnation of *Goddess Lakshmi*, the consort of Maha Vishnu, but this was not known to anyone in Mithila.

Although King Janak and Queen Sunaina had a younger daughter whose name was Urmilla, Sita was the *"apple of their eyes"*. At a very tender age while cleaning, Sita effortlessly lifted the Great Bow of Lord Shiva to the amazement of her father. At that moment, King Janak made a vow that whoever shall lift and string that Bow will marry his daughter, Sita. While this may seem unfair to Sita, her father wanted to ensure that his daughter marries a suitable match as we all hope for our children. In today's world, it might be wise for parents to help or guide their children to select a suitable life partner so that they can live happily in wedded bliss.

Back in Ayodhya, amidst the daily engagement of his Rulership, King Dasrath spent quality time with his young sons teaching them good *Sanskar* (upbringing) at a tender age. Soon the time came for the boys to be sent off to *Gurukul* or School. As advised by their Guru, Vashistha the most appropriate date to begin studies was selected. It was on the auspicious day of *Saraswati Jayanti* that the boys left the loving comfort of their home to pursue education. It is believed when important matters are undertaken on an auspicious date, it may yield a favorable outcome.

It was heartbreaking for the Queen Mothers and the King as well, parting from their young children for such a long time. In that, parents and their beloved children became reunited after their child's education was completed. That meant that a child leaves home to pursue an education around age 5 and returns home as a teenager. It was such a huge sacrifice for the King and his Queens, especially in light of how many years they longed to beget children.

Learning and discipline are fundamental areas of children's growth and development. In today's world, education is the gateway to all happiness and success in life, as *'knowledge is power and the magic formula'* towards the fulfilment of our goals and desires. Hence, the young boys proceeded with their Guru, Vashistha to his hermitage far away where they were taught about Vedanta, Science, Philosophy, Yoga, Meditation, Archery and other related Studies.

The wise Guru who possessed a far-reaching vision into the future also prepared the young boys for every hardship that may befall them as one never knows what is in store for them along life's journey. While they were engaged in tough lessons during the day, they were provided with tender love at night by the Guru's wife, Arundhati who sang lullabies to them and taught them Music.

With such a healthy balance of a child's learning and development, the boys were taught about caring and sharing, good moral and spiritual values, ethical behavior, and selfless service to others. They were also taught about tolerance and respect for others who are different in one way or the other. The wise Guru treated all the boys equally, regardless of who was rich and who was poor. In that way, the boys learned to appreciate others for who they are and what they are, and to not criticize others, but to appreciate and see goodness in all human beings.

As they toiled daily and begged for alms for survival, they were taught the critical importance of planting a tree, rather than deforestation, as well as engaging in sustainable consumption to help protect planet Earth. Although they came from a wealthy home, they had little to eat. Thus, they learned to conserve and not waste food, water and other basic amenities that is necessary for sustenance and survival. Similarly, we must also try to live more sustainably by not wasting food, water, power and so forth to help protect Mother Earth, and to also try to help others when possible in the name of humanity. Moreover, being a responsible citizen contributes to the Economy of one's country and thus, helps to provide for a more safe, healthy and equitable life that may help reduce crimes, inequality, inequity and poverty.

Hence, in that way, although Rama and his brothers were Princes, Vashistha ensured that there were no differentiation between them and the poorer boys. For instance, the Princes had to undergo the same harsh treatment as the poorer boys, such as performing daily outdoor chores and collecting alms. Thus, they learned to embrace differences and develop oneness with fellow human beings to avoid strife and to live peacefully and happily among mankind.

Many years passed in that way, then it was time for the Princes to return home. There was much jubilation among the people in the city of Ayodhya as the heirs of the *Sun Dynasty* arrived home. The Princes were given a purifying bath and were then dressed in their Royal attires as befitting of their status. The King and his Queens were so delighted at heart to behold their Princes and moreso, to have their dearly, beloved sons back at home.

Quite often, King Dasrath sneaked into Rama's room and stared at the sleeping Prince. Although Dasrath loved his sons dearly, Rama was dearest to his heart as he was truly the ideal son, and the very epitome of beauty and perfection. Thus, the King was so attached to Rama that he feared separation from his beloved son again. As parents, we can all relate to the unconditional love and attachment towards our dearly beloved children.

One day the renowned Sage, Vishwamitra visited the King and as is customary, the King went out and humbly greeted the Sage. After performing his worship and providing him with a most comfortable seat, the King inquired about the welfare of the Sage. Vishwamitra then stated that the purpose of his visit was to seek help from the King. Immediately, King Dasrath assured the Sage that whatever he seeks will be granted.

The Sage readily explained to the King that He and his disciples are unable to complete their *Yagna* (Sacrifice) as the demons, Marich and Subahu daily interrupts their *Yagna*. The demons, hovers over the altar and throws blood and bones into the Sacred Fire, thus dousing the fire that instantly halted the performance of the *Yagna* for human's welfare.

Vishwamitra continued, that though he possessed the Power to burn those demons to ashes, He explained to the King that such actions on his part are prohibited. That is to say, discipline in the performance of such rituals are essential to acquire the purpose of the Sacrifice. Thus, the Sage kindly asked for Rama and Lakshman to accompany him to protect His *Yagna*. The King was struck with fear and agony as his sons were mere boys and he doubted whether they could battle with such powerful demons. Moreover, the King could not bear separation of parting from his beloved sons whom he described as his *"two eyes"*.

The King begged of the Sage to leave his two young sons and to take him and the Royal Army of Ayodhya instead, but the Sage was firm in his resolve. Vishwamitra then reminded the King of his spoken word to give him whatever He asked for upon his arrival. The King was not left with an ultimatum and being a *man of his word*, he was thus, advised by his wise Guru to concede to Vishwamitra's request. Heartbroken, King Dasrath bid farewell to his sons, Rama and Lakshman as they left with the Sage.

On their way, they encountered a most powerful demoness in the forest by the name of Taraka. Rama effortlessly destroyed her with his prowess and powerful arrows. Subsequently, the Sage bestowed Rama with powerful, divine weapons. Having reached the ashram of Viswamitra, the Sages then commenced the performance of his *Yagna*, while Rama and Lakshman stood guard.

As expected, came the demons, Marich and Subahu. Rama shot and killed Subahu, and using a headless arrow on Marich, he was sent thousands of miles away to the *'point of no return'*. Thus, the Sages happily completed the rituals in peace and harmony. After that, the Sages continued their daily rituals, undisturbed with the protection of Rama and Lakshman.

Ram Sita Vivaah/Wedding

One day an invitation came to Vishwamitra from King Janak of Mithila to attend his daughter, *Sita's Swayamvar* (Engagement). The wise Sage informed Rama and Lakshman of the Grand Event, and they both happily accompanied the Sage to Mithila. On their way, they came upon an abandon ashram whereby, Rama noticed a *Tulsi Plant* that grew at the base of a huge stone, while other plants in the vicinity were all dried up. Thus, Rama inquired about the mystery of the *Tulsi Plant* being alive.

Sage Vishwamitra then explained that there once lived Gautam Muni with his beautiful wife Ahalia at that ashram. One day as Gautam Muni went out for his morning bath and rituals, the *Lord of the Heavens*, Indra who was lusting over Ahalia's beauty took the form of Gautam and went to the ashram to meet Ahalia. As Gautam Muni returned after taking a bath in the nearby stream, the disguised Indra came out of the ashram.

Ahalia then realized that she was tricked by the man in the disguise of her husband and wept bitterly. Conversely, Gautam was furious, and in his uncontrolled fury, despite how much his wife begged for his forgiveness, he immediately pronounced a *powerful curse* on her that instantly transformed her into that huge stone. Moreover, He cursed Indra to become impotent. Gautam departed his body and ascended to the Heavens.

The all merciful Lord Rama, who is the *"ultimate redeemer"* was then advised by Sage Vishwamitra to release Ahalia from the curse. Rama gently touched the stone with his *lotus-like feet*, and it was immediately transformed. There stood Ahalia with clasped hands and tearful eyes as she devotedly bowed in reverence and devotion to the compassionate Lord. Rama smilingly blessed her, and she ascended to Heaven to reunite with her husband.

As they continued on their journey to Mithila, Viswamitra took the Princes to the *Ganga* (river), whereby he narrated the descent of Ganga Devi on Earth. The narration goes back to the ancestors of Rama during the reign of King Sagar. During the performance of an *Ashwamedh Yagna*, the Sacred Horse went missing. Having unsuccessfully searched everywhere, the 100 sons of King Sagar from his first Queen proceeded to the Netherworld.

The horse was finally found close to the ashram of Kapila Muni who was deeply engrossed in meditation. Out of ignorance, the sons of King Sagar accused the Great Sage of stealing the horse. The Sage was awakened from his deep meditation, and in his fury, through his divine powers, he instantly burnt them all to ashes. When one falsely accuses and hurts an ardent devotee of God, one may suffer immensely for making false accusations, use of offensive words and evil actions.

The remaining son of Sagar from his second Queen came in search of his brothers. Having been told of their unfortunate demise by the Great Sage, Prince Abimanyu was grief-stricken and begged of the Sage for his forgiveness. He implored the Sage to advise him of a way to redeem the departed souls of his brothers. Kapila Muni then advised the Prince to perform austere penance to bring Ganga to Earth. Abimanyu tried and failed, but it was only a son of the third generation, Bhagiratha that was successful in his plea to bring Ganga to Earth.

Through Bhagiratha's austere penance, he firstly appeased Lord Brahma who advised him to propitiate Lord Shiva to help in the descent of Ganga to Earth. Hence, Lord Shiva accepted the flow of Ganga on his *jata* (nutted hair) as the impact of her powerful flow would have damaged the Earth. Thus, the flow of Ganga washed away the ashes of Bhagiratha's ancestors, and they were all purified and redeemed of their sins.

Sometimes the noble efforts and sacrifices of one person can bring about positive changes in the lives of people. Likewise, imagine the significant changes that can take place when people cooperate and collaborate to acquire a common good or purpose for the welfare of humanity. According to the Great Mahatma Gandhi, *"be the change you want to see in the world"* as change begins with an individual.

Having reached Mithila, Vishwamitra sat under the shady Mango Grove, while Rama and Lakshman after obtaining the permission of Vishwamitra went ahead to view the City. The City was beautiful beyond compare as is appropriate where the Universal Mother dwelled. The people of Mithila were spellbound as they gazed at the charming, uncomparable beauty of the two Princes. Rama who was dark in complexion and Lakshman who was fair. Being mindful of the condition laid down by King Janak for the prospective husband of their charming Princess Sita, they all wished that Rama would be successful to lift and string the Mighty Bow.

Having heard of Sage Vishwamitra's arrival, King Janak, his Guru Shatananda, and other Brahmanas went out and lovingly received the Sage with all honors. Shortly after, the two Princes, Rama and Lakshman arrived and took a seat next to Vishwamitra. King Janak emotionally fixed his gaze upon Sri Rama as if there were some connection or intoxification to that charming form that left the beholder spellbound. He then inquired of the gracious Sage about the identity of the Princes and was told that they were the sons of King Dasrath of Ayodhya. Viswamitra and the Princes were then escorted to a Chamber in the palace to rest.

After daily worship of the family's deity Lord Shiva, Sita and her companions were sent by Queen Sunaina to worship Girija Maata at a most *Sacred Shrine* in the Garden. Simultaneously, Rama seek permission from Viswamitra to fetch flowers for the sage's morning worship. Rama and Lakshman happily proceeded to the Garden as well. Incomparably beautiful was the Garden that produced flowers of different types and colors, as well as lovely creepers and plants that were a delight to the eyes.

At the well kept Garden, there was a lake at the middle where the lovely lotuses blossom. The sweet sound of the bird's chirping and the buzzing of bees as they sucked the nectar from the flowers filled the calm, cool atmosphere. Amidst all that, the beautiful Golden Temple of Girija Maata shone most resplendently. Both Sita and Rama were unaware of each other's visit to the Garden as the meeting of two loving hearts are destined by the Creator. Their innocent minds were absorbed in similar thoughts as they both went to the Garden for the purpose of worship.

As advised by her mother, Sita devoutly worshipped Goddess Girija in mind, body, and soul. One of her companions wandered away when she beheld the beauteous form of Rama and Lakshman in the Garden fetching flowers. She hastened to the temple to share the delightful news to Sita. The charming maidens then escorted Sita to the Garden, whereby she gazed on the handsome form of Rama. Likewise, Rama fixed his gaze upon the beautiful countenance of Sita.

It is said it was as if time had frozen for the divine pair that beheld each other for the first time after their descent on Earth, (*Rama was the incarnation of Maha Vishnu while Sita was the incarnation of his beautiful consort, Maha Lakshmi*). After receiving Rama in her heart through her beatiful eyes, Sita returned to the temple. Being respectful of her father's vow and honor, she silently expressed her heart's longing at the feet of Girija Maata, immensely praising the Goddess in many ways.

Girija was so pleased with Sita's humility and devotion that a *Mala* that adorned the bosom of the Goddess slipped and fell on Sita's head. Sita felt delighted at heart and the gracious Goddess smiled and spoke in sweet tones, assuring Sita that her heart's desire will be fulfilled. That meant, Rama will definitely be her husband. Sita was overcome with joy and repeatedly offered obeisance to the Goddess in gratitude, then happily returned home.

As she reminisced the beauteous form of Rama, Sita's mind was greatly perturbed as she recalled her father's vow pertaining to the strict conditions of her marriage. Simultaneously, Rama's mind grew restless being deeply absorbed in pure thoughts of Sita's charming and divine form. Later, upon arrival of Bharat and Shatrughna, Lakshman was too eager to share Rama's love story to the delight of their brothers.

Rama smiled lovingly at Lakshman's sweet innocence, and then enlightened his younger brothers about the sanctity of marriage. Rama strongly advised that a man must maintain his loyalty to his prospective wife which should strengthen after marriage as he should not think of another woman in his lifetime. Likewise, the woman also must remain faithful to her prospective husband and life partner. Such a sacred, strong bond that is shared between a wife and husband will survive any difficulties and challenges along life's journey like a firm rock that remains unshaken by a violent storm.

As we gather, the union of a man and woman is pre-destined by the Creator and solemnized on Earth. However, one must take the time to think, introspect and prayer for divine guidance on whether a prospective mate is right for us in every way that counts. Moreover, one must maintain decorum with regards to one's religious beliefs and social norms before any action is undertaken. In such delicate matters, we must not allow our heart to overpower our mind and brain. In that, based on a person's disposition, marriage can be the most important decision that one has to take in life, as it can either *add to* or *take away* from one's peace, happiness, and welfare.

Many Kings and Princes were invited to showcase their strength to string and lift the Great Bow and thus, marry the Princess. As the most charming Princess Sita was escorted to the assembly, all those gathered to participate in the Contest, were even more enthusiastic to string the bow being captivated by her charming beauty. Many tried and failed as they could not even lift the bow, let alone string it.

Some combined their strenghts to lift the bow, but yet failed miserably. King Janak grew worried and felt deeply disappointed and, in his anguish, he bitterly proclaimed that he was wrong to think that there were heroic Kings and Princes on Earth. He sadly added that had he known that, He would not have made such a silly vow that may deprive his precious daughter of Holy Matrimony. Thus, Sita may remain a spinster all her life, the King sighed.

As King Janak spoke thus, his perspective of warrior's abilities was intolerable for Lakshman who became angry and was unable to control his emotions. Lakshman stood up and addressed Janak's harsh proclamations by stressing on the great valor and exceptional strength of his brother, Rama. Rama silently indicated to his loving brother to return to his seat. Knowing the opportune time had arrived, the all-knowing wise Sage, Viswamitra smiled and spoke to Rama in soft tones *"Arise O' Rama, and relieve Janak of his distress"* according to Tulsidas.

Rama stood before the Bow amidst the taunts of the ignorant men in the Hall. Sita's mother Sunaina also expressed her doubts of a mere boy possessing the ability to string the Great Bow of Lord Shiva. However, her wise sister-in-law comforted Sunaina that *'one never knows where ability lies'*. Moreover, one never knows what the Lord has in store for us along life's journey as *"man proposes, but God disposes"*. Thus, there is always an underlining reason why things happen, both good and bad as what is meant for you, will certainly happen as destined.

Sita implored Ganesh, Shiva, and Gauri as she prayed that Rama will be successful in his attempt to lift and string the Bow. Rama looked around at the audience that appeared like painted pictures as they were all eager to see what will transpire. Rama glanced at Sita and perceived that she was in deep distress. Bowing to his Guru, and with a gentle smile on his lips, he paid obeisance to the Divinity present in the bow that is the Great Lord Shiva. Instantly, Rama effortlessly lifted, strung and snapped the bow to the amazement of all present in the large assembly.

The warriors were struck with awe and bewilderment as they could not comprehend the possibility of a mere boy accomplishing the tough task that even their combined efforts could not achieve. The thunderous sound of the breaking of the Bow resonated throughout the *Three Worlds* (Heaven, Earth & Netherworld) and immediately Parshuram was awakened from his deep meditation. He looked around anxiously and rushed to the location where that loud sound emanated.

Sita, her relatives and friends, as well as the people of Janakpur, were ecstatic that Rama lifted and strung the bow. Sita's mother, Sunaina then gladfully permitted Sita along with her companions to invest the beautiful garland on Prince Rama's bosom. They sang beautifully as Sita Devi walked slowly and shyly towards Rama. The most charming pair appeared as resplendent as a thousand lotuses in bloom to the eyes of the beholders at that special moment in time.

Rama & Sita – Most Charming Pair

Subsequently, Parshuram angrily arrived and spoke in harsh tones and bitter words, making inferences about Rama having broken the Mighty Bow of Lord Shiva. Brave Lakshman, as usual defended his beloved brother with firm, befitting answers to break the arrogance of Parshuram. Parshuram reacted aggressively, and in a fit of rage, he threatened to behead Lakshman.

Anger is like a dark shroud that blinds the mind's eye and intellect causing it to be devoid of clear thinking and good reasoning. This eliminates one's sense of critical thinking and good judgement of others and situations. Therefore, one must refrain from any actions or major decisions when angry to avoid causing pain and misery to oneself, and others - *emotionally, mentally and psychologically.* Such actions on the part of an angry person will definitely lead to regret and self-destruction. Similarly, one must not act in haste or when hurt or distressed as any decison taken in such a vulnerable state of mind may not be a wise choice.

Rama smiled and spoke respectfully in soft tones to Parshuram which dispelled his anger and made him calm, thus forced him to introspect, and to recognize the Divine Reality that stood before him. Having relinquished his anger, and employed his divine insight, Parshuram recognized Rama as the *Lord of the Universe, Maha Vishnu* and gracefully bowed in reverence to him, while seeking forgiveness. Parshuram bestowed his blessing upon all and peacefully departed.

Uncontrolled anger is the root cause of conflict and pain that can lead to remorse and self-destruction. However, if one approaches unfavorable situations with a calm mind and good sense, then appropriate solutions can be derived to restore peace of mind and happiness. We must always think before we speak or act, and moreso, in a conflicting situation, we must think more and speak less to avoid saying or doing anything that we may certainly live to regret.

A message with the wedding invitation was sent to King Dasrath informing him of Rama's display of strength and valor in breaking the Bow to marry Princess Sita. Dasrath and his Queens were elated on receiving the good news as Princes Bharat, and Shatrughna read the message aloud. The family Guru, Vashistha was consulted and the most auspicious date and time were chosen for the wedding procession to start on their journey from Ayodhya to Janakpur.

Delightfully, King Dasrath, Guru Vashistha, Bharat, Shatrughna and the Wedding Party arrived in Janakpur to the warm and hospitable welcome of King Janak and the Royal Family, Guru

Shatananda and the people of Mithila. Both Kings, their respective Gurus, other Brahmanas of both Parties and elders of both families, then sat in consultation regarding the wedding proceedings. King Janak and King Dasrath, two storehouses of virtue and humility immensely praised each other as one saw the other as the real beneficiary of the good fortune of the ideal union of Rama and Sita.

The learned Gurus and Brahmanas then suggested that it will be inappropriate for Rama to return to Ayodhya in wedded bliss, while Lakshman, Bharat, and Shatrughna return unmarried. Thus, the proposal was put forth by both Gurus for Lakshman to marry Sita's younger sister Urmilla, and for Bharat and Shatrughna to marry Mandavi and Shrutikirti respectively, who were the cousins of Sita and the daughters of Janak's younger brother, Kushadhwaja. The proposal warmly delighted the hearts of King Janak and his family, and with sheer gratitude, they readily and happily consented.

The Grand Royal Wedding of the four brothers took place amidst great pomp and celebrations. Moreover, Lord Bramha and Lord Shiva along with their consorts, Saraswati and Parvati respectively descended on Earth in complete disguise to bear witness to the wedding ceremony of Sita and Rama. As preparations were being made for the departure of the Grooms' Party, Sunaina held counsel with the four young brides as she bid them *'farewell'* with her final words. She advised the Princesses to stay true and faithful to their husband and to respect and cherish their in-laws as their parents.

It was now time for the young brides to depart to their new home. King Janak who was a pillar of strength and courage wept bitterly for the first time as he bid farewell to his beloved daughter, Sita. She was affectionately called Janaki because of the close father-daughter bond, and as such, she was by no doubt Janak's weakness. The wedding procession arrived in Ayodhya whereby, the Queen Mothers and the people were anxiously awaiting the newlyweds.

The people of Ayodhya sang and danced in ecstasy as it was a most joyful occasion. The young brides were warmly received by the 3 Queen Mothers, whose hearts were filled with love and joy as they beheld the charming four pairs.

On the wedding night, Sita requested of her husband to accept her as his humble servant. However, Rama disapproved of a wife being treated as a servant and requested of Sita to be his equal partner, and that she should not hesitate to correct him if he makes a mistake. Moreover, the loving Rama added that it is normal for a King to have more than one wife, but promised that she will be his One and Only wife. He stated that is his *Gift and Given Word* to Her as Mother Kaikeyi advised him that it is customary that the husband presents a Gift to his Bride on the wedding night. Rama, thus concluded that he took that vow on the first day he laid eyes on her in the Garden. Sita retreated in modesty as her innocent heart overflowed with love for her Lord Rama.

The Queens treated the new brides with great love and affection as if they were their daughters. Likewise, the Princesses respected and honored their husband's parents as their own as they exemplified the high ideals of their nuptial home. In that way, the young brides soon adjusted well to their new home where peace, love, bliss, prosperity, and happiness abounded.

When a daughter-in-law is treated like a daughter and likewise, a son-in-law is treated like a son with love by their in-laws, such a home will yield unity, harmony, prosperity, happiness, and success. Similarly, when a daughter-in-law or son-in-law, respect and honor their spouse's parents as their own, such a relationship will foster peace, happiness and eternal bliss.

Proposal of Rama as King

King Dasrath having recognized that he was much advanced in age then, decided to give up the throne to his eldest son, Rama. Thus, having consulted the idea with his Guru and Ministers, Rama was summoned to the Court. He was informed of the King's decision to crown him the new King of Ayodhya, but Rama reacted negatively. He felt that it was unfair for him to succeed his father as he would then acquire a higher status than his brothers who were born and married on the same day as him.

Both Dasrath and Vashistha explained to Rama in more ways than one that it was the right thing to do, as He was the eldest son and possessed all the right qualities of a righteous Ruler. That meant Rama was polite, truthful, knowledgeable, compassionate, selfless, and loved by the people of Ayodhya. Dasrath further explained that he felt most contented and accomplished that his sons are happily married, and his Kingdom is prosperous and moreso, His Subjects are also contented and living happily. So, after much deliberation, Rama conceded to his father's decision. Rama posited sometimes along life's journey, you may arrive at a crossroad whereby, you don't know which way to go or what is right and what is wrong.

Perhaps, we all can relate to such experiences in our lives. However, we must have confidence in the advice of our Parents and Guru or Teacher as based on their knowledge and life's experiences, they know what lies in our best interest. The news spread like Wildfire throughout the City of Ayodhya. The Queen Mothers, Bharat, Lakshman and Shatrughna, as well as the people of Ayodhya (*Ayodhya Vaasi*), were elated with the brilliant proposal. On the contrary, Manthara who was the maid of Queen Kaikeyi was annoyed at the idea of Rama ascending the throne.

An auspicious date was set, and all necessary preparations were being made for the Coronation of Rama as the King. Conversely, the Devatas in the Heavens were not in favor of Rama's Coronation at that particular time as the *'key purpose'* of his descent on Earth was yet to be accomplished. That is, Maha Vishnu had incarnated as Rama to rid the Earth of the atrocities of the vile demon, Ravan and other demons and to restore peace and happiness in the lives of the people. Also, many ardent devotees of Rama who dwelt in the Forest were patiently awaiting the *darshan* (sight) of the beloved Lord to attain *moksha* (liberation).

Therefore, the Devatas approached Goddess Saraswati, who is the Embodiment of Knowledge and Speech. Thus, she can dictate an individual's speech or action in accordance to her *Will.* The Devatas pleaded for her help to change the course of *Event in Ayodhya.* The merciful Goddess indicated that she will try to help as *only* Rama's *Will* prevails. Saraswati Maata influenced the mind of Manthara to persuade Kaikeyi to advocate the Coronation of Rama. In that way, Rama can proceed to the Forest to fulfil the burning desires of his Devotees, and to eradicate the evil forces.

Although the three Queens equally loved all four Princes, Manthara who was dull-witted by nature always favored Bharat over the other Princes. So when the news of the Coronation of Rama reached her, she became angry. Thus, she devised a plan to cease the Coronation of Rama, so that Bharat can be crowned the King instead. Manthara instantly hastened to Queen Kaikeyi's Chamber to execute her plan. However, unlike Manthara, Kaikeyi was thrilled with the idea of Rama's Coronation as she loved Him dearly as her son, Bharat.

Eventually, with a very high degree of effort, Manthara succeeded in poisoning the mind of Kaikeyi against Rama. Mathara finally was able to convince Kaikeyi, that with Rama being the King, She (Kaikeyi) would be like a slave to Kaushalya. Kaikeyi, who was the most charming among the three Queens and thus, Dasrath's favorite Queen could not even bear the thought of herself being demoted, so she readily succumbs to Manthara's cunning advice. Then, Manthara advised Kaikeyi to ask for the two boons that were promised to her by the King.

It goes back to many, many years when King Dasrath was engaged in fierce battle and fell unconscious due to injury on the battlefield. Kaikeyi immediately drove his chariot to safer grounds, thus saving the King's life, so He felt greatly indebted to Kaikeyi. Consequently, the King promised her two boons which she can freely request at any time. Manthara also advised Kaikeyi to resort to a pitiable state by casting off her Royal attire and jewelry. In that way, Manthara concluded the King would feel pity for her and thus, grant her unprecedented request. Kaikeyi fully heeded Manthara's advice and shifted to the '*Koob Bhavan*' which is a designated dark room in the palace whereby, one resorts to when one is angry or unhappy.

After a long day of planning and preparation for the Grand Event, Dasrath being delighted at heart proceeded straight to Kaikeyi's Chamber, but strangely noticed she was not to be seen. He then inquired from one of her maids and was shocked to hear that she is in the '*Koob Bhavan*'. The King hastened there only to see Kaikeyi, dressed in black and unadorned, lying on the floor in a most pitiable state. In soft tones, he inquired of his beloved Queen of the reasons for her sorrow, but Kaikeyi remained silent.

As advised by Manthara, she waited until Dasrath promised in the name of Rama, to give her anything she asked for before breaking her silence. As expected, Dasrath vowed in Rama's name to grant anything she desired to make her happy. He then requested that she returned to her Chamber and adorned herself beautifully to the delight of his eyes.

As the King desired, Kaikeyi was happy to fulfil his small request as she felt elated at heart that her scheme to secure Dasrath's pity was successful. She then reminded the King of the two boons he had promised her. Ignorant of her intentions, the King calmly inquired into what she seeks. Kaikeyi then asks for her two boons. Firstly, that Bharat is crowned King instead of Rama, and secondly that Rama is exiled for 14 long years. The King stood motionless and speechless hearing of the second boon as if his beloved Queen had pierced his heart with a dagger. He certainly did not expect her to ask for something that cruel, as banishing his beloved Rama to the forest for 14 long years.

Recovering himself, he begged of her to reconsider the second boon as he was willing to grant her the first boon, but she was firm on her resolve. Dasrath dropped to the ground and wailed and begged of Kaikeyi to not banish Rama, but she was not in the least affected by her husband's plea and distress. Instead, she started making a mockery of her husband's oath to uphold the high ideals of the Raghukul Dynasty *to give up one's life as necessary in keeping with one's given word*. Those taunts completely shattered the King that he grew faint with grief, trembling and unable to utter another word. In that most pitiable condition of the mighty *Lion of the Raghu house* (Dasrath), the hopeless, dark night moved on slowly, while Kaikeyi stood heartlessly.

It is already devastating when someone faces pain and sorrow along life's journey. Thus, we must try to pacify others in grief, not *add fuel* to their distress. If we are unable to help someone in distress, then we must not taunt or laugh at that person as life is strange and incomprehensible. Therefore, we must be continuously mindful of our words, actions and deeds, as one's plight today may be our plight tomorrow. Thus, let us act wisely to refrain from doing or saying anything that may hurt or add to the pain of others as adding *salt to injury*. Rather, we must try to apply a soothing balm to one's heartache in the form of love, comfort and compassion to help remedy another's plight.

Rama's Exile

Contrary to Kaikeyi's cunning behavior, Kaushalya spent her night in steadfast devotion, chanting the 1008 names of Maha Vishnu Bhagwan for the successful undertaking of her son's Coronation. At dawn, the Band started singing beautiful invocations to start the day right, but all music and songs were ceased at the behest of the King. At daybreak, strangely the King was not seen, so the Chief Minister, Sumant was summoned by Guru Vashistha to check on the King. It was then that Sumant saw the pitiable condition of the King, and having inquired from Kaikeyi the reasons for the King's grief, Kaikeyi instructed Sumant to fetch Rama immediately.

Rama hastened to Kaikeyi's Chamber at once and saw his father in such a deplorable condition. He inquired from his mother, Kaikeyi as to the cause of his father's grief. Kaikeyi stated she sought her two boons from the King and that is the reason for his condition. Sri Rama who is dispassionate politely further inquired, *'is that all'* to which Kaikeyi nodded. Rama lovingly assured Kaikeyi that he would happily honor her wishes and uphold his father's oath as he emphasized, *"blessed is the son who has the good fortune to fulfil the command of his parents"* (Sargar).

Kaikeyi felt delighted at Rama's selflessness, she was shocked that Rama took it in such good faith. In contrast, Dasrath was unable to utter a word as he was so weak with grief over the idea of parting from his beloved son. To fully fathom the pain and agony of one's distress, one must be placed in the same or a similar situation. In this context, Dasrath was not only pining for a beloved son, but separation from the Lord. Hence, *a life without God is like a fish out of water that will struggle for life and gradually die.*

Rama proceeded to his Mother's Chamber to seek her blessings, and to inform her of his departure to the forest. Kaushalya had just completed her devout worship and was delighted to see her beloved

Son. She gladly adorned her son's forehead with the *Sacred Tilak of Maha Vishnu* along with her blessings. Rama then revealed the news of his exile that struck her like lightning. It was such a harsh, severe blow that rendered her speechless, sadden and in disbelief. Oh, how she wept bitterly for her beloved son as what was expected to be a most joyful day for the Royal Family and *Ayodhya Vaasi*, (people of Ayodhya) had turned out to be the saddest day for all, except Kaikeyi and Manthara.

Kaushalya also wanted to accompany her son to the forest, but was opposed by Rama, as he explained at length her duty towards her husband. Soon, as the news quickly spreaded, Sita came by to verify the information. She also expressed her intentions to accompany her husband, but Rama disapproved of the idea. Out of concern, he stressed that she will not be able to handle the harsh conditions of the forest.

However, Sita strongly posited that her place is at her husband's side, wherever Destiny takes them. Rama tried in many ways to deter her, but she was firm on her resolve. Moreover, Sita turned to Kaushalya for support who advocated Rama's arguments as he had just lectured to Kaushalya about a wife's duty towards her husband. Thus, Rama was forced to concede and agree to take Sita along.

Subsequently, Lakshman came followed by his mother Sumitra and he also insisted on accompanying his brother to the forest. Rama tried to deter Lakshman as well because the exile was meant for Him (Rama) only. As such, Rama did not want his loved ones to suffer on account of Him. However, like Sita, Lakshman argued that life without Rama is meaningless and incomplete, as Rama is like both Mother and Father to him.

Rama was unable to defend the strong arguments put forth by his brother, Lakshman. Therefore, with the support and permission of his mother, Sumitra, Rama lovingly consented to take Lakshman along as well. Taking the blessings of both Kaushalya and Sumitra; Rama, Sita and Lakshman proceeded to acquire the blessings of the King before departing to the forest.

King Dasrath was still unable to contain himself, while Kaikeyi stood proudly at his side with her maid, Manthara. Rama, Sita, and Lakshman seek leave of the King, but a heart-broken Dasrath was too grief-stricken to utter a word. He was unable to bear separation from his beloved children. Worst yet, they were then presented with the garbs of hermits by a delightful Kaikeyi and Manthara, thus casting away their Royal Attire. Dasrath, choked with grief was unable to speak, but through body language, he indicated to his beloved Rama that he should not go to the forest.

However, Rama posited that it was his foremost duty to carry out the command of his mother while honoring his father's given word. Dasrath now realizing that he was unable to convince his righteous son to retreat, he tried to convince his beloved daughter-in-law atleast, to desist from going to the forest. However, like Rama, she was also firm on her duty by her husband to stand by him through good or bad, joy or pain. Thus, after taking the blessings of Guru Vashistha and King Dasrath, as well as Kaikeyi, both Princes and the Princess left the palace.

The entire city of Ayodhya wore a dismal look as Rama, Sita and Lakshman mounted the chariot to the shouts of '*victory*' to whom was proposed to be their "newly appointed king" that same day. The grief-stricken people of Ayodhya also wanted to accompany Rama to the forest to serve him. Although Rama in his sweet, loving tones tried to deter them, they were overpowered with love for him, thus they followed the chariot.

Meanwhile, as King Dasrath heard the shouts of the people as Rama, Sita and Lakshman departed, he dragged forth in his weaken state calling out to his beloved son Ram, but shortly collapsed. His

Queens rushed to his aid. However, he instantly denounced Kaikeyi and harshly accused her of ruining their happy home. Hence, with the loving support of Kaushalya and Sumitra, He took refuge in Kaushalya's Chamber (Sargar).

At nightfall, they reached the banks of the river Tamshe. Rama asked Sumant to dismount the chariot so that they can rest for the night. As the people were fast asleep, Rama awoke Sumant and whispered to him to mount the chariot. He advised Sumant to drive the chariot in different directions, so seeing the wheel marks, the people would be confused as to which direction they went. In that way, they will all return home to their families, and to the King. Besides, the exile was meant for Him only so why should the people sacrifice their happiness to suffer the calamities of the forest, Rama thought. Thus, Rama bowed in reverence to the Divine Souls of the people and proceeded on his onward journey.

As they went further into the forest, they came upon a Settlement of Forest Dwellers. Guha was the King of that tribe who was Rama's close friend from the days of Gurukul. Guha was so delighted to meet with his dear friend again, but was concern seeing Rama dressed as a hermit wandering in the forest. Upon inquiry, Rama related everything that transpired in Ayodhya. Guha, saddened by his friend's plight, offered his Kingdom to Rama, while his tribe presented Rama with fruits and vegetables for their sustenance.

Rama was touched by their hospitality and innocent love. However, he explained to his friend that though he was grateful for their love and support, he cannot accept anything. Rama further stated that according to the conditions of His Exile, He is not allowed to accept gifts from anyone, nor was he allowed to enter upon any City during the 14 years. Guha, though he understood, was grief-stricken by the harsh penalties that his dear friend had to endure and thus, offered his help to Rama in whatever way He deemed fit.

As they arrived at the banks of the Holy Ganga, Sita paid obeisance to Ganga Maata seeking her blessings and a safe return. Rama also sought Guha's help to cross the Ganga. Guha then summoned the boatman, Kewat who dwelt nearby. Kewat recognized in Rama, the *Lord of the Universe* and thus laid down a condition for Rama to mount his boat.

Kewat's humble request was to wash the feet of Rama firstly, and only then would Rama be allowed to sit in his boat. Rama was touched by the excessive love of Kewat and thus, fulfilled the desire of his devotee. Kewat washed Rama's feet and sipped the water as he worshipped the Lord who is the *'boatman that takes everyone across the ocean of life'*.

At that point, Sumant was advised by Rama to return to Ayodhya, but Sumant wanted to accompany Rama on his onward journey. Thus, Rama comforted Sumant's aching heart with the gentle words that His father, Dasrath who was also Sumant's childhood friend needed him more, now than ever. Sumant wanted to at least take Sita back, but she gently reminded him that her place was with her husband, Rama.

Sadden and disappointed, Sumant was left with no other option, but to return to Ayodhya. Kewat then took Rama, Sita, Lakshman and Guha safely across the Ganges. Sita offered to Kewat, Rama's ring as a token of appreciation, but Kewat refused to accept any payment. Rama smiled lovingly recognizing Kewat's unconditional love and devotion. Thus, bidding him farewell, they proceeded on their onward journey.

Meeting with the Rishis/Sages

They arrived at Rishi Bhardwaj's ashram. Bhardwaj was delighted at heart to behold the divine form of Rama who dwelt in his heart. Rama, Sita, and Lakshman were warmly received by the Sage. Rama then inquired of the Sage about a suitable place for them to reside. Rishi Bhardwaj advised Rama to settle in Chitrakoot amongst nature that is serene, divine and most beautiful.

Guha helped Lakshman to create a raft to take them across the river. Then, Rama gratefully turned to Guha as it was time for him to return to his Tribe (people), but He was saddened to bid farewell to his dearest friend, Rama. Guha wanted to stay in the loving company of Rama, but the Lord was firm in his resolve for Guha to return to his kin and people as their leader. Thus, Rama lovingly embraced and bid farewell to Guha.

We must not take undue advantage of another's kindness as one must only accept assistance when necessary. We must be mindful that others have a life of their own and as such, they have other vital duties to perform by their family, work, community and so forth. Therefore, we must strive to do things independently of others as much as possible as therein lies our self-esteem, success, learning experiences and development from which we build our strength, character, and wisdom to lead a righteous, healthy, prosperous and fulfilling life.

As Rama, Sita and Lakshman proceeded to Chitrakoot; they came across the serene ashram of Valmiki. Thus, seeking the blessings of the Great Sage, they proceeded on their onward journey. Having selected a most suitable spot, Lakshman constructed a Hut with sticks, twigs, and leaves in the beautiful vicinity of Nature whereby a beautiful stream flowed. Lakshman took care of every necessity to secure the comfort and welfare of his brother and *bhabi* (sister-in-law), despite their adverse conditions. He stood guard by them day and night, and never slept to ensure their safety and protection.

Meanwhile, Sumant returned to Ayodhya and upon seeing him alone, Dasrath's last hope of reuniting with his beloved son, Rama proved futile. Thus, with each passing day the King's condition deteriorated, and as he laid in bed, he recounted the chapters of his life, while constantly chanting '*Ram, Ram, Ram*'. As his last days grew near, he began hallucinating and calling out to Kaushalya, as he claimed to see the parents of Shravan Kumar and the *curse* they pronounced on him.

It goes back to when Dasrath was in his youth before his marriage. Daily he would venture into the forest to practice his archery skills. Prince Dasrath was an excellent archer who would hit the target without looking at it, but rather by just listening to the mere sound of something. It was on such a day; he heard a sound of something fetching water in the nearby river and blindly, he shot an arrow in that direction. As usual, the arrow met its target, but unfortunately, it was not an animal as he thought, but a human being that was struck. Consequently, when Dasrath heard the pitiable cry of a human being, he rushed to the scene, and there lying in a pool of blood was Shravan Kumar with an arrow stuck to his chest. Being a righteous person, Dasrath was terrified and felt remorseful for his unjust action of striking a harmless, and innocent human being.

Dasrath, choked with emotion and trembling as a result of his guilt and wrongdoing, begged Shravan's forgiveness. Shravan, gasping for breath, explained to Dasrath that he came to fetch water for his old, blind parents who were waiting nearby. He humbly requested of Dasrath to take the water for them to quench their thirst as it may at least save their lives. Shravan finally breathed his last as his soul departed. Dasrath, unable to face the harsh consequences of his actions, took the water to Shravan's parents.

At first, they were unable to recognize that it was not their son, as they were blind. However, they thought it rather strange that he was not replying to them, and thus realized that something was certainly amiss. They inquired repeatedly about the identity of the person that stood there in silence.

Dasrath in a deep state of remorse and sorrow handed the water to Shravan's father and then narrated the unfortunate incident that occurred. Hearing the awful news, Shravan's parents pronounced a curse on Dasrath that just as they are dying out of grief for their beloved son, similarly he will die grieving for his beloved son. With those words, Shravan's parents died due to extreme shock and grief. Likewise, Dasrath spent his last days grieving for his beloved son, Rama and thus succumbed to his grief as the soul left his body.

As scriptures declare, whether knowingly or unknowingly if one commits a mistake or wrongdoing, one must bear the consequences of it. No one is perfect, as such, we may sometimes unknowingly make a mistake, as to err is human nature and it is through our mistakes that we learn. However, I think to unknowingly make such a grievous mistake as Prince Dasrath in this scenario was pre-destined by the Creator. On the contrary, one must be mindful that when one knowingly or deliberately commits a heinous mistake or when a mistake becomes a habit, based on the pain incurred as a result of that mistake, then such a mistake may be unforgivable.

Unfortunately, the Ruler of the Raghukul Dynasty who was blessed with four powerful sons, was bereft of his sons' presence when he breathed his last. Rama and Lakshman were in the forest, while Bharat and Shatrughna were at Bharat's grandfather's place in a far-off City. Hence, upon the demise of the King, Guru Vashistha instructed Sumant to immediately dispatch a messenger to Kaikeya to summon Bharat and Shatrughna to return home. Moreover, the wise Guru warned that the messenger donot divulge the bad news of their father's passing to the Princes. In that, unexpected bad news or information may cause grievous harm to a person's mental and psychological health and general wellbeing.

That morning, Bharat awoke from a terrible dream about the demise of their father which He shared with Shatrughna. Bharat panicked as it is believed that dreams at dawn are likely to come true. Subsequently, being informed of the arrival of a messenger from Ayodhya, Bharat became terrified, and thus indicated to Shatrughna that he feared that something was certainly amiss at home. As instructed, the messenger only conveyed to the Princes that their Guru, Vashistha had summoned them home.

The palace wore an unusual, dismal look thus Bharat grew pale as he believed something was definitely wrong. Having met with their Guru Vashistha, they received the sad news of the passing of their father and all that had transpired preceding his unfortunate death. King Dasrath's body was completely covered in oil in a large container to preserve it as preparations were made for the final rites. The Princes were heartbroken to see their brave and powerful father in that pitiable state.

The Princes firstly visited Queen Kaushalya, whereby Bharat begged forgiveness of Kaushalya for being the wretched son of that woman that deliberately tore such a united and loving family apart. He also expressed his refusal to meet with his mother, Kaikeyi. Kaushalya tried to convince Bharat that no one was to be blamed as it was all the "will of destiny" at play. Thus, Bharat reluctantly proceeded to meet with his mother Kaikeyi at the behest of his wise, respected, elder mother, Kaushalya.

Kaikeyi, as she waited in anticipation was delighted to see her son. On the contrary, Bharat overcome with grief was filled of bitterness towards his mother which he expressed through his harsh words. Kaikeyi tried to explain to Bharat that she was only seeking his best interest, but to no avail. Hence, Kaikeyi was heartbroken as what she thought was in favor of her son, was now being held against her, as Bharat now saw her as an enemy of the family.

Moreover, Kaikeyi realized the grievous wrong she had committed, but it was too late to retain the peace and joy of the Raghu House. Simultaneously, Shatrughna followed the cunning Manthara and as he attempted to punish her, he was stopped by Kaushalya and Sumitra. Although Manthara was the mastermind that conspired to separate the brothers which led to the premature demise of the Great King, history holds Kaikeyi responsible as she was the one that implemented the grievous plan. However, enlightened souls like Kaushalya and Rama donot blame anyone as what was written by *Providence* was bound to happen.

After the final rites of King Dasrath was performed, Bharat sat in counsel with his Guru and expressed his desire of going to the forest to fetch his beloved brothers and sister-in-law. Knowing Rama to be duty-bound and true to his resolve to honor his father's words, the wise Guru dismissed the idea. However, Bharat insisted that even if Rama refused to return, then he will conduct the Coronation Ceremony right there, as Rama is now the rightful King of Ayodhya. Vashistha was touched by Bharat's ethical conduct and his deep affection for his brother thus, he endorsed the proposal. King Janak was also invited to witness the Coronation as a father figure. Hence, they all set forth on their journey with the Queen Mothers as well.

All along the way, after they inquired from place to place about the whereabouts of Rama, they arrived in Chitrakoot. Recognizing the Flag of the *Solar Dynasty* or the *Raghu House* from a distance, Lakshman who went out to fetch fire sticks hurriedly returned to inform Rama. Not thinking clearly, Lakshman inferred that Bharat and the army of Ayodhya came to slay Rama, so that Bharat would rule the Kingdom without fear. In Lakshman's ignorance and haste, he threatened to immediately attack and kill Bharat before he gets close to Rama.

Rama looked at Lakshman in utmost shock and then affirmed that Bharat has no such cunning intentions, as Bharat loves him dearly. Conversely, Lakshman ignored Rama's words and was firm in his resolve of what he believed to be the *truth of the matter*. Thus, as Lakshman stepped forth, a heavenly voice was heard affirming His power to destroy Bharat indeed, but warned that he would regret his wrongdoing. Thus, Lakshman retreated and controlled his fury, as he waited to find out the real reason for Bharat's visit.

Without taking the time to know and understand the reasons for someone's behavior or actions, we must not make inferences about others or cast judgment, based on what one perceives to be the Truth as one can be so very wrong. In this modern age, there will be no "voice" from the Heavens to stop us from undertaking a bad action or making a grievous mistake.

Rather, one should heed the "voice" from within in the form of our *Conscience* and *Soul,* as well as advice from those who are wiser and trustworthy. Perhaps, in that way we may protect ourselves from creating a blunder or grievous mistake that we may live to regret. Some mistakes may be unforgivable as in the triumph of jealousy, ego and anger when one realizes one's mistake of causing hurt and pain to an innocent being; it may be too late.

Soon Bharat and Shatrughna met with Rama, Sita, and Lakshman. Bharat was elated to *feast his eyes* on his beloved brother, and with tearful eyes, he embraced Rama. Rama also was pleased to see his brothers. It was such an emotional reunion of the brothers, then Rama inquired about their beloved father. Bharat sadly related the devastating news about the passing of the King. That shocking and awful news shook Rama like an arrow that pierced his heart.

As Rama tried to come to terms with the news, he laid eyes on Guru Vashistha, followed by the Queens. Rama was more saddened to see his beloved Mothers dressed as widows. With a grieving heart, Rama lovingly reached out and greeted them. Likewise, Sita and Lakshman reverently offered their respects to the Guru and Mothers. Guru Vashistha then offered wise counsel to the brothers and advised Rama and Lakshman to perform the *tarpan* (sacred) offerings for the liberation of the soul of their deceased father.

Later that day, Bharat communicated to Lakshman the purpose of his visit to perform the Coronation Ceremony of Rama. He asked Lakshman to hint the idea to Rama so that they may get an insight of Rama's reaction to his proposal. Rama immediately dismissed the idea as he was firm on achieving the purpose for which his exile was initiated.

Further, Queen Kaikeyi with a burdened heart filled with guilt for causing separation and distress to her happy family, as well as the untimely demise of her husband, approached Rama and begged his forgiveness. Rama lovingly pacified her stating that he does not hold her guilty for their situation as it was the *Will of Providence*. Nonetheless, Kaikeyi wept bitterly for hurting such a divine and noble soul as Rama. However, Rama never held Kaikeyi nor Manthara in contempt as he understood it was the *Will of Destiny*.

Camps were erected for the Guru, Mothers, Bharat and Shatrughna to pass the night safely and comfortably. The next morning, King Janak arrived with his consort, Sunaina. Sita was happy to meet her parents again. They all sat in council to discuss the Purpose of their visit. Bharat who is the very epitome of *Love* addressed his brother Rama indicating his desire to perform Rama's Coronation as He is now the rightful King of Ayodhya. Rama, however, dismissed the proposal as he was firm in his resolve to upkeep the promise of his father to Kaikeyi.

Duty triumph over Love

Bharat, overpowered with love and affection tried in many ways to convince Rama to return to Ayodhya, but Rama stood firm in the name of *Duty* to complete his 14 years exile. Bharat, overcome with love for his brother Rama, with tearfilled eyes, He beseeched Rama again and again, but to no avail. He then turned to Guru Vashistha for support, but though the Guru was moved by Bharat's loving entreaty, he was also unable to convince Rama in Bharat's favor.

Although Rama was touched by Bharat's innocent love and humble request, he maintained his *Stand* as not only was Rama honoring his father's promise to Kaikeyi, but also upholding the high ideals set by his Ancestors. Rama further explained that the time was not right for him to accept the *Throne,* nor return to Ayodhya, and moreso, it would not *bring back* his father. Thus, Rama added that he has to perform his *Duty* to the best interest of all concerned in keeping with the *Raghukul Dynasty's Honor and Prestige.*

Bharat, thus recognizing that he is prolonging a losing argument, with clasped hands and tears streaming down his cheeks, he turned to King Janak in supplication. King Janak being a father-figure to the Princes, was deeply touched by the loving entreaties of both, Bharat and Rama, however, he completely understood both sides. Unable to utter a word or take a *Stand* in this delicate, sensitive matters of the heart and mind, King Janak an ardent devotee of Lord Shiva, invoked the blessings of the Lord for *Divine Guidance.*

Praising Bharat for his unconditional love for his brother that will be written in History, and Rama for standing firm by his Duty, Janak broke his silence. He emphasized that one must rise above one's emotions to perform one's Duty, as therein lies the ultimate challenge of a Great Soul. In other words, in this peaceful, sensitive, strong arguments between *Love* (Bharat) and *Duty* (Rama), Duty triumphed over Love.

Thus, Rama fulfilled the desire of Bharat by accepting his proposal to be the King of Ayodhya, but humbly requested of Bharat to rule the Kingdom until his exile is completed. Rama added, that upon returning to Ayodhya after 14years the Coronation Ceremony will take place in Ayodhya. Bharat lovingly accepted, but requested Rama's wooden sandal to be placed on the *Throne* in his absence. Rama, being greatly touched by his loving brother's pure love and humility, readily obliged. Bharat placed the wooden sandal on his head, in tears he took a final gaze at Rama, then left with his group.

Having reached Ayodhya, Bharat placed Rama's wooden sandal on the *Throne.* Giving up all Royal comforts; Bharat governed the affairs of Ayodhya through his Guru, brother Shatrughna and the Ministers. Moreover, subjecting himself to the conditions under which his beloved brother lived, he also dressed in the garbs of a hermit and stayed at a hut in Nandigram, the outskirts of the City.

Treating himself as a servant to his Master Rama, he dug a pit, and that is where he slept as he believed that a servant's dwelling place should be beneath his Master. Such was the brotherly love of those storehouses of virtue in the form of Bharat and Rama, all in the name of Duty. In that way, Bharat passed the time in the absence of Rama. Moreover, Kaikeyi's first boon for Bharat to be King, rather than Rama, was fulfilled. Simultaneously, Rama upheld his principles to fulfill Queen Kaikeyi's second boon, thus honoring his father's promise, as well as his highly reputable lineage.

Settling in Panchavati

Rama thought it was not wise to reside in Chitrakoot anymore as everyone in Ayodhya knows about their whereabouts. Therefore, Rama, Sita, and Lakshman proceeded further into the forest. They came upon the ashram of Atri Muni and Anusuiya Maata. Anusuiya was that blessed wife who performed unwavering devotion to her husband during His *Tapasya* or austere penance.

Consequently, she won the favor of the Devatas who respectfully bestowed upon her divine gifts of clothing and jewelry. Those gifts she lovingly presented to Sita whom she considered as a daughter. She also imparted good counsel to Sita that staying faithful to her husband and being the delight of his eyes is the foremost duty of a *'pativrata naari'* or a devoted & faithful wife. Likewise, Atri Muni also imparted divine knowledge to Rama and Lakshman.

Rama was spellbound when he saw his charming wife adorned beautifully with exquisite jewelry and ornaments. The unique sari given to her by Mother Ansuriya was one that would never become dirty or soiled. Taking leave of Atri Muni and Mother Ansuriya they proceeded on their onward journey. Next, they arrived at the ashram of Sharbhang who was eagerly awaiting the sight of Lord Rama to depart the world. After beholding the beauteous form of Lord Rama, the Sage attained *moksha* or liberation.

As Rama, Sita and Lakshman proceeded deeper into the *Dandaka Forest*; they came upon heaps of bones being the remains of the Sages that were mercilessly killed by the demons. Having seen that, Rama felt immensely hurt and thus, solemnly declared to destroy the demons and restore the Earth and its people to happiness, love, peace, and unity. Rama then met with Sage Sutiksha who was delighted at heart to behold the charming form of the Lord whom he worshipped daily. Next, Rama met with Maharshi Agastya who bestowed upon Rama divine weapons as a means to combat battle with the powerful and cunning demons.

As they continued on their journey, they met with a huge vulture bird, named Jatayu. As Rama introduced themselves, Jatayu communicated that King Dasrath was his childhood friend, so he consider them to be like his children. He further added that he has a brother, named Sampati, but unfortunately, they got separated. Rama was delighted to have met a dear friend of his father in his time of adversity. Thereafter, they came upon a most beautiful and peaceful vicinity called Panchavati. Hence, selecting an appropriate spot with the flowing stream nearby, they built a hut and decided to reside there for the remaining time of the exile.

Finally, it was the last year of Rama's exile. One day, as Lakshman went out to fetch firesticks, Rama seized the opportunity to speak to his beloved consort in private. He informed Sita that the time had come for them to achieve the *key purpose* for which they had descended on planet Earth *(as previously stated, Rama was an incarnation of Maha Vishnu, the Sustainer of the Universe, while Sita was an incarnation of his beloved consort, Maha Lakshmi).*

Rama cautioned Sita that it was going to be the most difficult time for her, and that she needed to be strong. He further advised that she remained in the custody of Agni Devata and leave her shadow image behind. Sita lovingly heeded her husband's wise counsel and thus, invoked the *Fire God,* and humbly requested His kind favor. Agni Devata was pleased to be of divine service to the Lord of the Universe, Rama and the Universal Mother, Sita. Thus, Agni Devata accepted the *"real Sita"* leaving behind her illusionary form, as advised by her Lord Rama. Lakshman was not aware of this as he was not present at that time.

One day, Shurpanakha, the sister of Ravan, the King of the demons, was wandering through Space when she beheld the most charming form of Rama. Instantly, being captivated by Rama's incomparable beauty, she longed to have him as her mate. Hence, she descended and through her magical powers, she adopted a beautiful form, and approached Rama. Trying to entice Rama with her sweet words and charm, she claimed to be the most beautiful woman, while Rama is the most handsome man and thus, they should marry.

Sita who was incomparably the most charming and beautiful female form emerged from the ashram. Rama politely informed Shurpanakha that he is already happily married. She then glanced at Lakshman and approached him with her proposal. Lakshman also rejected her which made her very angry. Her immense anger revealed her true form, and she rushed towards Sita in a fit of rage to attack her. Shurpanakha assumed Sita was the reason for the Princes disapproval of her proposal. As Shurpanakha attempted to attack Sita, Lakshman instantly slashed Shurpanakha's nose, thus crushing her ego and false pride.

Shurpanakha hastened back and provoked her demon brothers, Khar and Dushan whom immediately went forth with their army of demons. They were certainly no match for Rama's strength and valor and thus, Rama effortlessly destroyed Khar and Dushan along with their army. Not getting the satisfaction that she expected, Shurpanakha then proceeded to Ravan and lamented in his Court.

She took advantage of Ravan's ego for beautiful women to satisfy his lust as she described the incomparable beauty of Sita. Thus, she provoked Ravan to go after Sita. She never revealed the truth of the matter to Ravan that resulted in her ugly nose, but rather instigated him to go after Sita. Nonetheless, hearing of Sita's incomparable beauty, Ravan's longing to possess her grew stronger. Hence, he decided to devise a plan to kidnap Sita.

Subsequently, Ravan mounted his flying chariot and landed at the ashram of Marich, who was once shot by Rama with a headless arrow, and had since then transformed his life. Marich possessed the immense power to adopt any animal form that he desired. Thus, informing Marich of his plan to kidnap Sita, Ravan suggested that Marich took the form of a *golden dear* to entice Sita.

Marich was leading a *Holy life* to atone for his sins and thus, was not interested in engaging in any sinful actions. Moreover, he had already experienced the wrath of Rama and heeded that as an awakening call. Thus, he tried to explain that in a subtle way to Ravan, but Ravan was self-centered and thus, determined to have whatever he wants even though it belonged to someone else.

Finally, Marich advised Ravan to not incur enmity with Rama as no one can withstand Rama's prowess, but Ravan dismissed the wise counsel of Marich as he claimed to be most powerful. At that point, Ravan became very angry and thus, threatened to kill Marich if he refused to carry out his command. Marich concluded that his death is inevitable. In other words, if he refused to act, Ravan will kill him, and if he acted as Ravan advised, then Rama will kill him. Hence, he cleverly chose to obey Ravan, so that he can be killed by Rama and thus, attain liberation, as a result of dying at the divine hands of Lord Rama. Sometimes in life, in challenging or compromising situations, one must first think and then wisely speak or act, to avoid making inappropriate or poor choices and bad decisions that may lead to pain and suffering.

Sita & Rama's plight

It was a most beautiful day as the early morning sunlight filled the serene atmosphere to the chirping of birds. Sita was delightfully gathering flowers for worship from the Garden closeby, when she heard a jingling sound. Looking up, she feasted her beautiful eyes on a fascinating golden deer. Captivated by its beauty, she hastened back to the ashram to inform Rama of that delight of her eyes. She humbly requested Rama to catch the deer, so that they can take it back to Ayodhya as a unique momento of their forest life. Rama smiled within himself, while Lakshman warned his brother that it might be a trick by the demons.

Sita however, longed for the deer and insisted that Rama catch it. The loving Rama who fulfills the desire of all instructed Lakshman to stand guard in his absence to protect Sita. Rama took leave and went after the deer. All along, the vile demon Ravan hid behind the bushes gazing at the most charming and beautiful countenance of Sita which *added fuel to his lust* to possess her.

As Rama chased behind the deer, it lured him further away and deeper into the forest as it was an illusionary deer, that was Marich in disguise. Alas, Rama shot an arrow that pierced the deer, thus revealing its true identity as Marich. Moreover, Marich mimicked Rama's voice and cried out to Lakshman for help. Rama realized that Lakshman was right and immediately hurried back.

Meanwhile, Sita hearing the screams of what she believed to be Rama's voice, requested Lakshman to rush to his brother's aid. Lakshman however, paid no heed as he knew there were no power on Earth to combat his brother's prowess, so how then could he be hurt or injured. His firm belief he communicated to Sita, but she was not keen on listening to Lakshman's good judgment. Instead, she politely pleaded with him to leave at once to assist Rama, but Lakshman stood motionless as he paid no heed to her.

When Sita realized that Lakshman was not at all alarmed of what she perceived to be her husband's distress, she spoke in bitter tones as she made a mockery of Lakshman's bravery. She continued to deride his valor and threatened to go in search of her husband if Lakshman chose to be a coward and stay at the ashram. Lakshman bent on following his brother's order had to give in to his sister-in-law's demand, as she became adamant to go instead. Invoking the protection of the Gods and mentally begging forgiveness from Rama, he drew a line in front of the ashram and advised Sita not to cross it under any condition. He then left in search of his brother, Rama. Sometimes, along life's path, what is meant to happen, despite precautionary measures taken to avoid it, will eventually happen as per the *will of destiny*.

Ravan, who hid behind the bushes and witnessed it all, smiled cunningly, as he now saw an easy target. Transforming himself into an aged *Saint* or *Priest*, he approached the ashram. He called out for alms, but Sita in a saddened state being completely absorbed in deep thoughts of her beloved husband heeded not his call. He called again, and then recollecting herself she greeted him and proceeded inside the hut to fetch something for him to eat as is customary.

As Sita went in, Ravan tried to cross the line drawn by Lakshman but was unable to, as sparks of fire emanated from it like an electric wire. Then, Sita came out with some fruits which she offered to the disguised Ravan, while staying within the confines of the line drawn by her brother-in-law, Lakshman. Mindful of his intentions, the vile demon refused to accept the alms, as he requested that Sita step over the line as a way of paying her respect to a *"Holy man"*.

Ravan then stepped back and sat comfortably in Rama's meditation seat outside. Heeding Lakshman's warning, Sita hesitated to cross the line, but Ravan threatened to pronounce a curse on Rama if she refused to concede to his request to offer the alms. He further added that he could see Rama was injured from the horns of a deer and thus, his curse will cause Rama his life due to her obstinacy.

An emotional and terrified Sita feared that the *Holy* man's fury and her refusal to cross the line may result in her husband's death, thus she stepped over the line drawn by Lakshman. When one crosses the line of one's cultural beliefs, one may become vulnerable to the evils and dangers of the world. The cunning demon Ravan felt delighted at heart and only then accepted the *alms* (fruits). He then inquired about her identity as He pretended not to know Sita. Thereafter, he started praising her beauty which Sita perceived was rather disrespectful on the part of a Holy man. Sita's mind became doubtful of his physical appearance.

Ravan pitied her condition and advised her to seek shelter from a wealthy man such as Ravan. Immediately, Sita recognized that he was not a *Holy* man, but a wicked demon. She demanded that he drop his disguise and reveal his true identity. The lustful Ravan revealed himself to a most terrified Sita who tried to run inside the ashram. However, Ravan mockingly reminded her that she crossed the line of protection already. Sita was devastated as she realized her grave mistake and the deceit of the vile demon. Ravan forcibly grabbed Sita and delightfully took her away on his *Pushpak Viman* (flying chariot).

Meanwhile, Rama hurriedly on his return to the ashram shockingly saw Lakshman approaching him. Lakshman begged forgiveness of his brother explaining the reason for his disobedience. Rama then explained to Lakshman that he was right, the deer was not real, but the disguise of the demon Marich. Immediately, both brothers grew concerned about Sita's safety and wellbeing and rushed back to the ashram.

Having reached the ashram, as they feared, Sita was not seen. They looked everywhere including at the nearby river, but she was not found. Grief-stricken, Rama wept bitterly for his beloved wife, Sita as he called out repeatedly to her. He and Lakshman, who equally shared in his brother's distress traverse the forest in search of her. Rama overwhelmed with grief through separation from his beloved consort asked the plants and the trees if they had seen his Sita.

As Ravan carried Sita away in his flying chariot, Sita also called out to her beloved husband for help as she wept bitterly. On hearing her screams, Jatayu, the vulture bird came to her rescue. Sita saw a ray of hope as Jatayu fought with Ravan, but he was no match for the powerful demon. Nonetheless, Jatayu combated fiercely with Ravan until the cunning demon drew his sword and chopped off Jatayu's wing, and he fell to the ground. Bleeding profusely, Jatayu chanted '*Ram, Ram, Ram*' hoping to behold the *Darshan* (sight) of the Rama before taking his last breath.

Sita noticed some monkeys sitting at the base of a mountain so she quickly removed some jewelry that was given to her by Mother Ansuiya. She tore the edge of her sari, bundled it and dropped it. She kindly requested the forest dwellers to present it to her Lord, Rama if they see him. She further added that they inform him that the wicked demon Ravan has abducted her. Although Sita was so terrified being abducted by the vile demon Ravan and grief-stricken over separation from her beloved husband, she thought cleverly. By removing and dropping her jewelry on the way, she hoped Rama may have a lead on which direction she was taken.

Those precious gems were not of any value to her when it comes to her love for her husband. She held her husband in such high esteem that nothing and no one came before him in her life. Afterall, she was wedded to the noblest and virtuous of all men. Likewise, Rama was wedded to the most charming and virtuous of all women in the world. What an ideal match! In this age and time, one may not find such a compatible partner in life, but after careful thought and consideration of choosing the most suitable life partner, one must respect each other's feelings and perspectives, and thus peacefully compromise where necessary to make their union, right!

As Rama and Lakshman wandered through the forest in search of Sita, they came upon the wounded, pitiable Jatayu. Rama lovingly lifted Jatayu closely to his bosom and inquired about his severe and painful condition. Jatayu related everything that transpired in his battle with Ravan in an effort to save Sita. Advising Rama to rescue Sita and to protect the dignity of his lineage, Jatayu breathed his last. Rama with his own loving hands performed the final rites of Jatayu and granted him liberation.

Having reached the Golden City of Lanka, Ravan kept Sita at the beautiful *Ashoka Vatika* which is the Royal Garden of his Kingdom. He sanctioned many demonesses there to guard Sita. Sitting under the Ashoka tree, Sita in utmost grief contemplated in her heart and mind the beauteous form of her Lord, Rama.

Although the mighty Ravan was a vile demon who was lusting over Sita's beauty, he never used force on her while under his captivity. He left her in the Garden as a means of giving her time to willing accept him. Afterall, he was born of the Bramhin race and was also a devout worshipper of the Great Lord Shiva. However, he allowed his greed, ego and vices to take control of his senses and in the process, destroyed countless innocent lives.

Rama killed the demon Kabandha as the search continued for Sita. Next, they came upon a most exquisite pathway covered with fresh flowers. Looking ahead, they noticed a very feeble lady sorting the flowers and aligning them nicely on the path that led to her ashram. Her name was Shabari who grew old nicely arranging a flower path and selecting sweet fruits daily for her Lord Rama. She held on to the firm belief that Rama would visit her as prophesied by her Guru, Matang Rishi before departing to the Heavens.

Recognizing his devout devotee, Rama walked slowly towards her. Shabari, deeply engrossed in creating that beautiful array of flowers suddenly noticed the appearance of Rama's lotus-like feet before her eyes. Having inquired of his identity, she prostrated at the feet of the Divine Lord that dwells in her heart and mind. Tears of love, devotion, and joy fell from her eyes washing the *lotus-like feet* of Sri Rama. Her heart throbbed in ecstasy over the fulfillment of her long-awaited burning desire, as she fixed her weary, teary eyes on the beauteous form of the Lord, Rama.

Composing herself, she lovingly took the Princes into her humble hut. She happily prepared a most comfortable seat for Rama, while Lakshman stood at his side. She offered to Rama the luscious fruits she had collected that morning. Moreover, she bit into each one to ensure that it was sweet before offering it to the Lord, Rama. Rama, being touched by the depth of her pure, innocent love and devotion lovingly partook of the fruits offered to him. Rama also shared fruit with Lakshman, but he refused to partake of it as Shabari had bitten into it.

After Shabari worshipped Lord Rama in that way, Rama narrated his plight to her. She advised him to seek help from Sugriv, the King of the apes. She then took Rama to the sacred spot outside, under the banyan tree whereby, her Guru Matang Rishi used to sit in deep meditation. Rama bowed in reverence to the Divinity that was still present there as a result of the austere penance of the Great Rishi. With her heart overflowing with pure love and devotion, Shabari requested enlightenment from the Lord. Rama who is the fulfiller of all heart's desire then lovingly recited the nine forms of devotion as follows according to Tulsidas (Sargar).

1. Good relationships with the Saints
2. Love for listening to the glories of the Lord
3. Unselfish service to the Guru

4. Singing the Lord's praises with devotion
5. Repetition of the Lord's name with unwavering faith
6. Self-control & being detached from manifold activities
7. High regards for the Saints and to see God in all creations
8. Contentment
9. Simplicity and Nobility

Rama also stressed that the Lord does not recognize a person by their caste, riches or fame, but the bond of devotion that a devotee cherishes in one's heart for the Divine Lord. Shabari's joys knew no bounds as Rama partook of her offerings and bestowed His Grace upon her, regardless of knowing she belonged to the untouchable caste. Rama smilingly blessed Shabari who then departed to the Heavens with a glad heart.

In the Hindu Caste System, *untouchables* are the lowest caste. As such, no one gives or accepts anything from them, nor is anyone allowed to help them. In the eyes of the Lord as Rama declared, no one is rich or poor, nor is anyone higher or lower, as the Lord sees every individual as being *Equal.* However, the Lord sides with those who uphold *Truth* as Bhagwan Krishna pointed out to Arjuna on the battlefield of *Kurukshetra.* In the same vein, Lord Krishna also stated that a lie that is spoken to serve the righteous cause is more or less equal to a hundred truths (Bhagwat Gita).

Hence, we must not discriminate or disrespect other human beings as everyone, regardless of religion, color, caste, and socioeconomic status deserves respect and justice, as there should not be any such barriers among the human race. Thus, we must reach out to others where possible and lend a helping hand to those in need, not for monetary gains, nor name or fame, but to serve the common good in the name of Humanity.

Meeting with Hanuman & Sugriv

Rama and Lakshman journeyed further to meet with Sugriv and his army. In a restricted cave on the mountain lived Sugriv with his host of monkeys including the mighty and powerful Hanuman, who was an ardent devotee of Rama. As Rama and Lakshman proceeded in that direction, one of the monkeys spotted the two brothers and immediately informed their Master, Sugriv. Being fearful that the Princes may be an enemy, Sugriv called on Hanuman. Hanuman was known for his intelligence, unmatched strength and bravery, so Sugriv instructed him to meet with the Princes to find out about their identity.

The wise Hanuman thought for a moment that if those guys turned out to be an enemy, then they may recognize him. In that way, they would be aware of Sugriv's location which may prove detrimental for Sugriv and his army. Hence, adopting the disguise of a Brahmin, Hanuman approached Rama and Lakshman and inquired about their identity. Rama spoke in sweet, loving tones that they are the sons of King Dasrath, and they are in search of his beloved consort, Sita who had been abducted by the vile demon, Ravan. Next, Rama politely inquired about Hanuman's identity. Hanuman became highly emotional, dropping his disguise, he adopted his real ape form.

With hands clasp and tearful eyes, he dropped at the sacred feet of Lord Rama in humble supplication begging for Rama's forgiveness. Hanuman felt remorseful as taking on a disguise form pretending to be whom he was not; He was unable to recognize his Lord Rama who is enshrined in his heart. Rama understood it all and smilingly and lovingly lifted and blessed Hanuman.

Hanuman advised that the path to the mountain was quite rocky, so adopting a gigantic form, He lifted Rama and Lakshman on his shoulders, and flew swiftly to the Cave to meet with Sugriv. Sugriv was informed of Rama and Lakshman's identity and their purpose. Hearing about the abduction of Sita, Sugriv retrieved the small bundle that was dropped by Sita which was brought by some of his apes. The small bundle was presented to Rama for him to examine closely to identify whether or not, it belonged to Sita.

Rama immediately recognized the piece of torn cloth from Sita's sari and then looking at the jewelry; He turned to Lakshman for verification. Lakshman however, only recognized the *payal* (foot chain) as that of Sita as he stated out of respect, He only looked at his *bhabi* or sister-in-law's feet. On beholding Sita's belongings, Rama became very emotional and vowed to rescue her at all cost.

Sugriv narrated his plight to Rama as well. Sugriv stated that they were two brothers, Him and Bali who though in the forms of apes were very strong and powerful. Bali, the elder brother, was the King of the ape race, while Sugriv was second in command. One day a powerful demon challenged Bali to combat battle. Going into the Cave where that demon resided, Bali advised Sugriv that he should wait outside the Cave.

Bali added that if after 30 days he failed to return, that Sugriv should conclude that his brother had been killed in the battle. Therefore, Sugriv should return home as the new King of Kiskinda, Bali advised. After 30 days, and seeing the blood flowing through the opening of the Cave, Sugriv feared that his brother Bali had been killed by the demon. Fearing for his own life, Sugriv panicked and closed the opening of the Cave with a huge rock. Further, that was the given instruction by his brother Bali, as such, Sugriv returned to Kiskinda, whereby He occupied the Throne.

Sometime later, Bali miraculously returned to the surprise of all, including Sugriv. Delighted at heart to see Bali again, well and alive, Sugriv gladly approached his brother. However, Bali was furious and started verbally abusing and physically assaulting Sugriv. Bali did not allow his brother, Sugriv to explain himself nor did he recall his final advice to his dear brother. As Bali continued to punish his innocent brother, a fearful Sugriv quickly ran away to save his life. Sugriv then settled in that mountain Cave along with his trusted apes, while unfortunately, his wife was kept forcibly in the custody of Bali. Sugriv felt safe in that cave as that particular mountain was restricted to Bali upon a curse from a Sage.

Rama and Sugriv forged an alliance with the proposal that Rama would help Sugriv *retain* his Kingdom and wife, while Sugriv and his army would help Rama to search for Sita. Thus, in the presence of the ape army, Rama and Sugriv initiated the bond of their friendship by circulating the Holy Fire as witness. As critical as Rama's plight were to rescue his beloved Sita, he gave priority to his friend's plight. However, Sugriv was doubtful as to whether the delicate Rama could defeat the most powerful Bali.

To eliminate his doubts, Sugriv showed Rama seven palm trees that were straightly aligned. He challenged Rama that if he can dispatch the seven palm trees by striking one single arrow, then he will be convinced that Rama possessed the strength and ability to destroy Bali. Rama smiled, and with one swift arrow all seven trees were dispatched, thus dispelling Sugriv's doubts. Rama advised Sugriv to challenge Bali to battle.

As advised by Rama, Sugriv called out to Bali to engage in battle. However, Sugriv was severely beaten by Bali, and thus fled the scene. Sugriv thought Rama had deceived him, but Rama confessed that both brothers looked identical and therefore, he was unable to tell them apart. Rama then invested a garland on Sugriv's bosom to be able to identify him, and advised Sugriv to resume battle with Bali the following day.

As Bali and Sugriv engaged in fierce battle, Rama shot Bali with his unfailing arrow. Bali dropped on the ground and looking up; he saw

Rama. Bali's wife Tara and his son Angad quickly arrived and were devastated to behold Bali's awful end. Bali accused Rama of killing him through deceitful means and questioned whether his action was right for someone of his lineage and caliber. Sri Rama listened attentively while Bali expressed his dissatisfaction.

Hence, Sri Rama reminded Bali of his many misdeeds, including the grave injustices done to his own younger brother, Sugriv. Rama further questioned Bali about where his good judgment of right and wrong laid, when He committed all those cunning and sinful acts. Bali was forced to reflect on his own life and realizing his mistakes, He begged forgiveness from both, Rama and Sugriv.

Bali advised his brother Sugriv to rightfully ascend the throne and to give due consideration to the advice of his (Bali) wife, Tara as she always offered good counsel to him. He also advised his son Angad to accept fellowship with Rama and be his servant, as therein lies his happiness and good fortune. Rama consoled a grieving Tara and Angad with enlightening words of wisdom and comfort. Rama instructed Lakshman to assist with the preparations for the final rites of Bali to be performed.

Rama anointed Sugriv as the new King of Kiskinda. Delightfully, Sugriv felt most grateful to his friend, Rama for keeping his oath. Rama allowed Sugriv time to reunite with his family and kinsmen. Moreover, as it was the rainy season, they decided to commence the search for Sita after the monsoon season was over. Meanwhile, Rama spent the time a Cave with Lakshman.

After the rainy season was over, it appeared as though Sugriv had forgotten to keep his promise, as Rama waited patiently for him. Rama was forced to send Lakshman to inquire about the delay of the cooperation and collaboration of Sugriv and his army to help find Sita. Lakshman hastily proceeded to Sugriv's place and angrily demanded to meet with Sugriv to remind him of his promise to

Rama. Sugriv surrendered at the feet of Lakshman and begged his forgiveness. He confessed being absorbed in the pleasures of his reign and family unity, he lost track of time.

Sugriv immediately summoned his army and together with Rama and Lakshman they engaged in discussion of potential ways and means to locate Sita. Rama, who is all-knowing and compassionate asked everyone to contribute their ideas. In that way, they all felt that sense of belonging that each one is important to the team and that their idea matters. It was decided that four groups be formed so that they can cover the four Cardinal points that is, East, West, North and South.

The stronger apes headed each group, thus dividing the strength of the army as they had no lead as to where Ravan resided. The group that proceeded South was headed by Angad and included the bear Jambavant and the wise, mighty Hanuman. Rama gave his ring to Hanuman as he felt Hanuman would be the one to meet Sita. Thus, when Hanuman meets with Sita and shows her the ring, she would recognize that Hanuman is His messenger, Rama thought.

Hence, as that group proceeded to the South they came across an enchanted, most beautiful Cave with lots to eat and drink. A Divine Lady, Swamprabha resided there. After satiating their hunger and thirst, she appeared and transported them to the Seashore through her divine powers. They were now very confused about moving ahead and they felt hopeless about how to cross the vast Ocean. However, they were determined to find a way to accomplish Rama's work. As they sat together in consultation, brainstorming ideas, they drew reference to Jatayu and how he was able to serve Lord Rama until his last breath.

A huge vulture bird, Sampati who was sitting nearby atop his Cave overheard their conversation and thus, inquired about Jatayu. It turned out, Sampati was the older brother of Jatayu. Sampati then related that he and his brother Jatayu contested flying to the Sun. As it became hotter, Jatayu retreated. However, Sampati through his ego to defeat his brother sallied forth. The burning rays of the beaming Sun scorched his wings and he fell atop that Cave unable to fly again.

Sugriv and Jambavant narrated Rama's plight and their mission to Sampati. Sampati through his eagle-like vision looked across the Ocean and saw Sita sitting under the Ashoka Tree in the Royal Garden. After hearing that, it was now a matter of who can cross the vast Ocean to reach Sita. Hanuman stood quietly as being absorbed in deep thoughts. Jambavant stated that he is too old to make the trip, while Angad opined that he can go, but may not be able to return. Consequently, all expectations were pinned on the mighty, brave Hanuman to undertake that impossible task of going to Lanka.

They all turned to Hanuman in supplication, while Jambavant, being the oldest and known for his wisdom, reminded Hanuman of his great valor, strength and infinite powers. As a child, Hanuman demonstrated incomparable wisdom and strength as he performed miraculous deeds. For example, one day He flew towards the Sun and swallowed it taking the Sun for a fruit. The entire world became dark, thus Lord Indra, who is the King of the Heavens struck Hanuman with the thunderbolt. Hanuman fell unconscious to the ground.

Subsequently, all the Devatas then begged Hanuman's father for Hanuman to quickly release the Sun for the welfare of the world, but Hanuman's father, Kesari put forth a condition. He stated that, firstly all the Devatas blesses his son of which the Devatas willingly obliged. Agni Devata blessed Hanuman that fire will not burn him, while Lord Indra blessed Hanuman that he would have everlasting life.

Further, similar to Baal Krishna who broke the pots and daily stole the *markan/dahi* from the milkmaids, Baal Hanuman was abit mischievous as well. As the Rishis sat in *tapasya* (meditation), Baal Hanuman would daily disturb them by playing tricks on them. For example, through his divine powers, he would lift them up and down in a playful manner, thus interrupting the meditation of the Holy Men.

Moreso, one day, Baal Hanuman threw the Rishi's Shiv Lingam into the river. That was the limit of his naughtiness, and thus the Rishis pronounced a curse on him. They proclaimed that he would be devoid of all his Divine powers until such time when he will need it. Moreover, they added that whatever He threw in the water will float and not sink.

In that way, the wise Jambavant related it all to Hanuman and as proclaimed by the Holy Men, the opportune time arrived whereby, Hanuman needed to reclaim his powers. Miraculously, Hanuman chanted the Lord's name *'Jai Sri Ram'* and started to grow in size. His huge body shone resplendently as numerous Suns combined as written by *Tulsidas*. Thus, Hanuman adopted a gigantic form and took a huge plunge as he embarked on his mission flying over the Ocean.

It was not smooth sailing for him though, as he met with obstacles on his journey. He encountered Surasa who wanted to swallow him, but through his intelligence, Hanuman defeated her. Subsequently, he encountered and destroyed Singhika, while being determined to accomplish his Master's work. In that way, Hanuman went forth without fail.

Hanuman's meeting Sita

Lanka, the *City of Gold* as was commonly known was beautiful beyond description. As Hanuman arrived in Lanka, he adopted a tiny form and tried to enter the main gate, but stopped by Lankini. Lankini was a demoness who stood guard at the main entrance to Lanka. She was carefully chosen to occupy that position by Ravan.

Ravan was informed by Lord Brahma upon receiving his boon, that whenever Lankini would be defeated, it will be a sign that his end is near. Lankini was also aware of this, so when she tried to stop Hanuman from entering the City, Hanuman gave her a severe blow, and she dropped to the ground. Thus, she immediately recognized the Divinity in Hanuman and begged his forgiveness.

Having entered Ravan's palace, Hanuman who had never seen Sita before and thus, had no idea of her physical appearance, searched for her from place to place. He saw Ravan comfortably asleep, as well as his charming wife, Mandodari. Although Mandodari was also a virtuous lady and most beautiful in appearance, Hanuman doubted that she could be Sita. Hanuman reasoned within himself that a faithful wife who is separated from her husband would not be comfortably asleep in luxury. Thus, using his critical logic in that way, he continued his search.

At dawn, he heard someone chanting the glorious name of '*Rama*'. Eager to know who can be so brave to chant the name of the Lord in the City of demons, Hanuman came upon Vibhishan's house. Hanuman was more surprised to see the *Holy Tulsi Plant* growing there and moreso, Rama's sacred name nicely written on the wall of Vibhishan's house. As Hanuman stood there observing, the noble Vibhishan came out wearing the sacred tilak of Maha Vishnu that adorned his forehead.

Greeting Vibhishan in the name of Sri Rama, Hanuman introduced himself as well as the purpose of his visit. Likewise, Vibhishan also introduced himself as the younger brother of Ravan which amazed Hanuman to a greater extent. Vibhishan then informed Hanuman that Sita was kept in the *Ashoka Vatika* (Garden with lots of Ashoka trees). He also advised Hanuman to approach with caution as many demonesses were stationed there to guard Sita.

At dusk, Hanuman proceeded to the Garden where Sita was kept. Peeping over the high walls, he felt delighted at heart to behold the most charming and divine form of Sita. She sat motionlessly with her gaze fixed in Space as though sinking into the bottomless Ocean of despair. Such was her pitiable condition being separated from her Lord Rama that she grew more and more despondent and pale with each passing day.

Hanuman undoubtedly recognized Sita as her divine form spoke of her identity of being the beloved wife of Rama. As the demonesses gathered to light their torch as dusk fell, Hanuman quickly jumped over the huge wall. He quietly climbed up the same tree whereby, Sita was sitting deeply absorbed in thoughts of her Lord, Rama.

To the sounds of the trumpets came Ravan followed by his wife, Mandodari and his entourage. As Ravan stood before Sita, she angrily turned away from him, and quickly upheld a blade of grass to represent a wall between herself and Ravan. Ravan smiled at her innocence and disposition lusting his gaze on her incomparable beauty. Again, he expressed his love and longing to possess her. Ravan boasted of his wealth and bravery as compared to other Kings as he claimed to be the greatest and wealthiest of all men in the Universe. Moreover, He stressed that Sita will be most happy as his Chief Queen.

Conversely, Sita in harsh tones, unhesitantly, dismissed his claims with befitting answers. She bravely argued that Ravan is a beggar in comparison to her husband, Rama who is indeed the Divine Lord of the Universe. Moreover, she questioned whether that was his so-called bravery when he abducted her like a thief in the absence of her husband and brother-in-law. In that regard, Sita stressed that Ravan took her away forcibly as a jackal, since he was afraid to face the *two powerful lions* of the Raghu House in the form of Rama and Lakshman.

Sita's harsh words pierced Ravan's ego like a dreadful arrow that significantly triggered his anger and fury. In that fit of rage, he drew his sword to behead her, but stopped by his noble wife, Mandodari who offered him words of good counsel. She advised Ravan that Sita is a guest in Lanka, thus it will bring him infamy for a mighty King like him to kill her.

Strangely, Ravan heeded his wife's advice at that time and gave Sita one month to accept him. He warned that if she refused to accept him within that time frame, he will behead her. Thus, ordering his guards to torture Sita to a greater extent so she may concede to his offer, he left angrily and disappointed. The demonesses abused and threatened Sita to consent to their King's desire, but Sita was devoted to her husband in thought, word and deed, mind, body and soul and thus, preferred to die rather than accept another man. The head lady, Trijata who was very kind to Sita and treated her like a daughter cautioned the other demonesses to stop torturing Sita.

Trijata narrated to them of a dream she had about the destruction of Ravan and the City of Lanka. She advised the demonesses to be kind and respectful to Sita, and honor her as therein lies their protection and wellbeing. All the demonesses begged forgiveness of Sita and prostrated before her. Hence, Trijata who was a devotee of Lord Shiva comforted Sita and advised her to have faith and pray to Lord Shiva, as her Lord Rama will certainly come to deliver her from her distress.

A tearful Hanuman felt the deep distress of Sita, as he witnessed it all seated on a branch as He hid between the leaves of the tree. As the demonesses fell asleep, Hanuman recited *Rama's Katha* to Sita as he recaptured significant events of Rama and Sita. Sita listened attentively and looked around eagerly, but saw no one in sight. Subsequently, Hanuman dropped Rama's ring before her eyes. Immediately, recognizing the ring she delightfully picked it up and then anxiously called out repeatedly to the unseen messenger to reveal himself. Hanuman jumped down from the tree and stood before her, but seeing his ape form, Sita felt disappointed as she thought it was another trick of the demons.

Consequently, Hanuman tried to convince her of his true identity as that of the messenger of Rama, but Sita sadly turned away as she refused to believe him. Hanuman requested of Sita to carefully examine the ring as it was the same ring that she presented to Kevat after safely crossing the Ganges. Sita was convinced and believed Hanuman, as the demons are not aware of that event. More so, she felt delighted at heart that someone finally came to her aid. She curiously inquired about her husband's well-being, and asked Hanuman to humbly convey her sincerest apology to Lakshman for crossing the line drawn by him on that day.

Hanuman reassured Sita that Rama will definitely come to deliver her from her plight now that he knows where she is kept. However, Sita expressed her concern that Ravan's army consisted of powerful demons and wondered if the ape army would be of any match to combat the demons in battle. Hanuman convinced her that there are many powerful warriors among the apes as well. Thus, he grew 85 feet tall reassuring Sita of the might and strength of Rama's army. Sita was convinced and felt delighted at heart.

With Sita's permission, the clever Hanuman proceeded to enjoy the luscious fruits in the Garden. As it was nighttime, all the guards were fast asleep. Thus, Hanuman deliberately went about plucking the fruits in a noisily manner and uprooted some trees to provoke the demons. It was a deliberate attempt to test the strength of the enemy. Hence, as expected the demons awoke and a battle ensued between the vile demons and Hanuman. Effortlessly, the mighty Hanuman conquered Jambumali and other demons in battle. Then Ravan's younger son, Akshay Kumar came forth whom Hanuman slew without much effort.

Hearing the terrible news, Ravan was devastated. However, his elder son, the mighty Indrajeet, assured his father that he would capture that monkey (Hanuman) who had been creating havoc in the Royal Garden. Ravan, despatched his son, Indrajeet who proudly and confidently took leave of his father to accomplish the task. Indrajeet was also a most powerful warrior who had once defeated and captured the Lord of the Heavens, Indra and was thus given that name. However, it was quite a tough challenge for Indarjeet to capture the mighty Hanuman. Hanuman used his intelligence to quickly evade the fast speed, striking weapons. As Indrajeet's arrows failed to defeat Hanuman, Indarjeet finally discharged the *Brahmastra* (the most powerful weapon of Lord Brahma – the Creator of the Universe). Recognizing the divine weapon of Lord Brahma, Hanuman bowed in reverence to it and thus, allowed himself to be bounded by it as a means of respect to Lord Brahma.

Indrajeet, unaware of the truth of Hanuman's surrender, beaming with ego and pride over his victory, took Hanuman in bondage to the Royal Court. Ravan was extremely delighted of his son's victory and congratulated Indarjeet. At the same time, Ravan was shocked to see that an *"ordinary monkey"* had put them to task by creating such havoc in the Garden, and was also responsible for slaying his younger son. He gazed at Hanuman from head to toe and then inquired of his identity. Hanuman gladly introduced himself as the *Messenger of Sri Rama*, and He was sent to warn Ravan of the consequences of his actions by abducting Sita and thus, creating enmity with Rama.

Hanuman advised Ravan to return Sita as Rama is the Lord of the Universe. Thus, failure to oblige to Rama's advice will result in a catastrophe for him (Ravan) and the people of Lanka. Ravan being very egoistic in nature, laughingly dismissed Hanuman's good counsel. Rather, Ravan boosted about his powers and unmatched strength to conquer the world. To shatter Ravan's ego and false pride, Hanuman also spoke of Rama's infinite powers and glories which immensely annoyed Ravan.

In his anger and fury, Ravan abruptly ordered that Hanuman is killed. However, the noble Vibhishan, his younger brother, advised that it is unethical to kill an envoy as Hanuman is the Messenger of Rama. Thus, heeding Vibhishan's advice, Ravan ordered his guards to set Hanuman's tail on fire as monkeys are very fond of their tail. The demons were delighted as they wrapped Hanuman's tail with pieces of cloth to set it ablaze. They poked Hanuman and made fun of him. Hanuman, being so simple and humble also smiled with them, and playfully kept extending his tail.

Consequently, the demons had to gather a lot of fabric to keep up with wrapping Hanuman's tail which made them very tired. What they thought to be a simple task, became a difficult one for them as Hanuman was not an ordinary monkey. The demons thought that they could have easily inflicted grievous harm to Hanuman, but He was a Divine Being and was also protected by Lord Rama.

Finally, Hanuman's tail was set ablaze and he gleefully leaped unto the air. He flew from one rooftop to the other setting almost all of Lanka on fire, with the exception of Vibhishan's house. The demons ran around in panic and distress as they tried to put out the fire to save their belongings and homes. Ravan stepped out in his balcony looking at the mass destruction done by Hanuman. His most pious, devoted wife, Mandodari again cautioned her husband to rethink his decision about keeping Sita. She emphasized that *"if the mere servant is so powerful to create such a disaster to Lanka, then how much more powerful is the Master"* (Sargar).

Hanuman who was blessed by Agni Devata that fire would not burn him, then refreshed himself in the nearby Ocean and proceeded to meet with Sita. Sita Devi who heard everything was delighted to see Hanuman safe and well. Finally, as Hanuman took leave of Sita, he requested that she also gave him a token for Rama. In that way, Rama would be convinced that He actually met with her. Barely left with any ornaments, Sita took off her *chudamani* (hair ornament) and gave it to Hanuman.

She kindly requested Hanuman to convey to her Lord, Rama that if he donot rescue her within a month, he will not find her alive. That was unfortunately the time frame Ravan put forth for her to accept him. Hanuman offered to take Sita along with him, but Sita being a most devoted wife stated that it would be contrary to her rectitude to willing touch another man. Moreover, she wanted Sri Rama to acquire the glory of rescuing her. Hanuman completely understood and bowed in reverence to the Divine Mother, Sita. Further, it must be noted, that Hanuman was only instructed to search for Sita, not rescue her.

Sita stood with a saddened heart as it was time for Hanuman to depart. She blessed him that his return journey be safe and free from obstacles. She also blessed Hanuman that he would never grow old and he will always be dearest to Sri Rama. Grief-stricken, Sita who finally saw a ray of light in her time of distress through Hanuman's presence, then bid farewell to him. Hanuman advised Sita not to lose hope as Rama will undoubtedly come to her rescue.

Meanwhile, 3 of the four groups that were dispatched to search for Sita returned unsuccessfully. Therefore, all hopes were pinned on the last group that proceeded to the South. As the sound of *'victory to Rama'* was heard from afar, everyone at the Cave were hopeful that good news were underway. Rightfully so, Angad happily returned with his group to the delight of all and Hanuman narrated his experience of meeting with Sita. Hanuman tearfully conveyed Sita's message to Rama that brought tears to his eyes and extreme pain to his heart. Lakshman also felt sad hearing of his sister-in-law's deep distress.

Hanuman presented to Rama the hair ornament given to him by Sita, which Rama recognized as the jewel he decorated her hair with on their wedding night. Rama lovingly clasped it to his bosom as his aching heart knew no bounds. Separation from his beloved Sita and now hearing of her most pitiable condition was unbearable for Rama. Recollecting himself, Rama lovingly looked at Hanuman with affection and gratitude. He declared that Hanuman is as dear to him as Bharat.

Hanuman, overcome with unconditional love for the *lotus-like feet* of his Master dropped at Rama's feet in loving supplication to the Lord. As much as Rama tried to lift him, He would not arise like that special moment in time froze for the dearly, beloved devotee, Hanuman. Lord Rama, recognizing Hanuman's deep affection and devotion towards him, thus stroked the hair of Hanuman lovingly. Lord Shiva in *Mount Kailash* also felt that display of love of Rama to Hanuman, as Hanuman was the 11th incarnation of Lord Shiva.

Rama consulted with Sugriv and the rest of the army, and they set forth on their march to the seashore. Having arrived at the seashore they were faced with the immense challenge of crossing the vast Ocean. Rama and his army deliberated on how to cross the Sea, as the merciful Lord Rama did not want to employ any harsh measures out of concern for the Ocean Habitats.

Rama & his Army arrives at the Seashore

Through a subtle approach, Rama decided to immerse himself in a three day meditation to appease the Sea God, Varun Devata to seek his help to cross the vast Ocean. However, Lakshman opposed the idea as he reminded his brother that time is of the essence to rescue Sita. However, Rama firmly emphasized that *'man's duty is to act and God's duty is to reward man's action'*. Therefore, we must perform appropriate actions to achieve our purpose in life. In other words, we must do everything in our power that is morally and ethically right to achieve our goals, as beyond that lies in the hands of the Lord.

After the three days passed, Varun Devata did not reveal himself, so Rama was forced to implore a different approach. He drew his arrow and threatened Varun to dry up the vast Ocean as a means to cross the Sea. Instantly, Varun appeared with clasped hands and begged for Rama's forgiveness. Varun advised the construction of a bridge to Lanka and promised to bear the force of it so that the army can cross safely.

We must always pursue our goals in a civilized way to avoid hurting or harming anyone or anything in the process, as well as to develop and maintain good, strong relationships. If necessary, using force within ethical boundaries should always be a last resort based on time, situation, place, and what needs to be accomplished.

The two architects of the army, Nal and Neel along with the host of bears and monkeys started the construction of the bridge. When the rocks were thrown into the water, they sank, but when Rama's name was written on the rocks and then placed into the water, the rocks stayed afloat. Such was the binding effect of the Lord's name that made possible an impossible task, through faith and devotion of devotees like Hanuman and others. It was a most amazing and beautiful display of teamwork to accomplish that most challenging task.

Simultaneously, Rama felt the urge to perform Shiva puja. Thus, constructing a beautiful *Shiv-lingam* out of sand on the Seashore, Rama performed steadfast devotion to Lord Shiva. Lord Shiva was very pleased and blessed Rama to be victorious. Meanwhile, the mighty Hanuman was about to lift a humongous rock when he was told that no other materials were needed. Thus, leaving the huge rock behind, Hanuman heard a strange voice emanating from that rock. The rock begged of Hanuman to take him as well so that he could be of service to the Lord.

Hanuman hastened to Rama and communicated the mystery of the huge rock. Rama smiled and instructed Hanuman to convey his message to Goverdhan Baba (the humongous rock). Hanuman then conveyed to Govardhan Baba that the Lord in his following *avatar* (incarnation) as Bhagwan Krishna would utilize that rock. Thus, as *Bhagwat Katha* extols Rama who is forever true to his word indeed kept his promise to Goverdhan Baba as explained below.

After the return of Sri Rama to his divine abode, thousands of years later, Maha Vishnu (who incarnated as Sri Rama), manifested as Bhagwan Krishna in the home of Nanda and Yashoda. One day, Lord Indra became very angry with the people of Vrindavan for deviating from their normal performance of his *pooja*/worship. He showered continuous torrential rains and thunderstorms with the intention of destroying the village. That servere weather resulted in massive flooding in the village which proved disastrous for the people and animals to find a way to save their lives.

The people turned to Sri Krishna for help and the Lord delivered by lifting the '*Govardhan Parvat*' or mountain with his little finger for seven days and nights to save the people and animals of Vrindavan. Thus, recognizing the immense power of the Lord as Sri Krishna,

Lord Indra descended and prostrated at the feet of Lord Krishna and begged his forgiveness. Such was the compassion of the Lord that He did not use Goverdhan in the construction of the bridge to walk on him. Rather, the Lord gave him an exalted position holding Goverdhan in high esteem above his head.

Now that the bridge was completed, Rama and his army to the chants of *'Har Har Mahadev'* crossed the vast Ocean successfully to Lanka. They carefully set up their camps and engaged in further discussion and planning. Ravan was shocked having heard the news from his spies that Rama and his army had reached the shores of Lanka. The good news also reached a grief-stricken, Sita through the chief demoness, Trijata, whom Sita honored as her mother in her times of despair. Once again, Sita saw a ray of hope as she prayed to the Universal Mother, Bhavani for the victory of Rama and his army.

In Lanka, King Ravan called a council with his Ministers. Vibhishan advised Ravan to return Sita and surrender to Rama. That aroused Ravan's fury as swollen with ego and arrogance; he angrily refused to accept defeat from anyone. He was bent on keeping his pride intact to acquire whatever he wishes, even through immoral and unethical means. Vibhishan, with folded palms, knelt before his elder brother, Ravan and pleaded again and again, to seek refuge in Rama as He is most compassionate and would pardon his selfish misdeed. However, Vibhishan's polite and wise counsel triggered Ravan's anger, and in his rage, he kicked Vibhishan and threw him out of the Kingdom.

Heart-broken, Vibhishan revealed his feelings to his mother who advised him to try one more time to persuade Ravan to return Sita. Thus, incorporating his mother's advice was the final attempt by Vibhishan to safeguard his brother's life, as well as the welfare of the people of Lanka. Unfortunately, it was of no avail as Ravan was firm in his evil ways to get what he wanted. Insulted and humiliated once more by Ravan, and feeling dejected, Vibhishan left to seek refuge at the lotus-like feet of Lord Rama.

On spotting Vibhishan, Sugriv and the army were doubtful of his intentions as it may not be wise to trust someone from the enemy's side. However, Rama who is always merciful and compassionate to the downtrodden, recognized the love, humility and devotion in Vibhishan's heart and offered him protection. Moreover, Rama anointed Vibhishan, the New King of Lanka. Although Vibhishan was the younger brother of the King of Lanka, as a Minister of the Government he was also responsible for the protection and welfare of his people. Hence, after many unsuccessful attempts to persuade an egoistic King to abandon his selfish motives and act towards the wellbeing and protection of his people, Vibhishan acted in the best interest of saving his innocent people. Thus, He was forced to seek help as he cleverly turned to the most capable person that is, Rama.

Mandodari begged her husband Ravan to surrender to Rama, but to no avail as Ravan was determined to maintain his ego. Ravan sent his spies, Shuka and Sarana to Rama's camp to find out about Rama's next course of action. The two spies, though in disguise were immediately recognized by Vibhishan who reported them to Lakshman. Thus, Lakshman took the most terrified spies to Rama. However, the compassionate Lord Rama forgave them as he understood that they were only carrying out the command of their King, Ravan.

Rama, Lakshman, Sugriv and Vibhishan surveyed the outskirts of Lanka and though from afar, the palace of Ravan was visible. At that very moment, Ravan was in his balcony and having laid eyes on him, Sugriv felt enraged over the plight of his friend, Rama and took a huge leap and wrestled with Ravan. However, it was not Sugriv's call to defeat Ravan. Thus, the defeated Sugriv was no match for Ravan's strength. A true friend is one who will share our pain and would stand by us in times of distress and is ever ready to help fight our battles in life.

Rama and Ravan arrange their respective armies to combat battle. However, the all merciful Lord, Rama thought of the safety and welfare of the people of Lanka. That is, all the innocent people who would be destroyed in the war. Moreso, the number of children that would lose their fathers, as well as the many wives that would lose their husbands. Thinking thus, the Lord decided to give Ravan one more chance for a peaceful settlement to avoid the war. Thus, Rama sent the youthful, but powerful Angad to Ravan's Court with his message.

Angad arrived at Ravan's Court as a messenger from Lord Rama's side. Since he was not offered any form of hospitality, he firstly created a seat for himself. He extended his tail to a significant length while curling it in a remarkable circular shape, thus creating a seat higher than that of Ravan's Throne. To the amazement of Ravan and all, Angad sat comfortably and introduced himself as the servant of Rama and the son of Bali. Hearing thus, Ravan tried to instigate Angad against Rama being the slayer of his father, Bali. However, the wise Angad did not heed Ravan's negative influence, as his dying father Bali had himself entrusted him (Angad) in the loving care of Rama.

As they engaged in dialogue, Angad tried to convince Ravan to act right and to return Sita to Rama, just as Hanuman, Vibhishan and Mandodari advised. However, as usual, the lustful Ravan became very angry and harshly dismissed Rama's message. Finally, Angad decided to take a Stand and threw a challenge for all the Ministers of Ravan. Angad firmly planted his right leg on the ground and declared that if any of Ravan's men were to shake or lift his leg, then Lord Rama will accept defeat and leave Lanka. This act by Angad is of high significance of our innate willpower to take a Stand to serve the righteous cause in confronting situations.

All Ravan's Ministers and Commanders including his mighty son, Indrajit came forward in an effort to lift Angad's leg, but none was successful. Feeling humiliated by this significant, shameful failure, an infuriated Ravan slowly walked towards Angad. However, just as Ravan attempted to hold Angad's leg, Angad moved away, and Ravan fell. Angad then affirmed that the trial was not meant for the King, and thus, again advised Ravan to surrender at Lord Rama's feet instead.

Thereafter, Ravan's maternal uncle, Malayavan and Mandodari's father, Mayadanav offered good counsel to Ravan to accept, and correct his mistake and surrender to Rama. However, Ravan heeds not the sound advice of anyone including his wise, caring relatives. Further, Ravan's mother, Kaikesi tried to convince and reason with Ravan that it is in the best interest of all concerned, including himself to return Sita and thus evade the war.

However, Ravan was bent on his way of satisfying his lust and ego, regardless of the pain, suffering and distress that his stubbornness cause to others. Mandodari again begged her husband to surrender as she claimed to have bad dreams about the destruction of Lanka. Unfortunately, Ravan was too proud of his strength and powers to heed the good counsel of those who genuinely cared for him.

Rama versus Ravan in battle

Upon Angad's return to Rama's camp, both Rama and Lakshman praised Angad and commended his bravery. With that being the last call by Rama for 'peace talks' with Ravan, the Lord and his army were not left with an ultimatum, but to unfortunately prepare for war. Both armies assembled on the battlefield and Rama addressed his army in sweet, polite tones as a caring father to his children. Rama's army chanted '*Har, Har, Mahadev*' in praise of Lord Shiva, as they proceeded forth, while Ravan's army of demons chanted '*Jai Lankeshwar*' in praise of Ravan, as they combated on the battlefield. When we put God foremost in every righteous action we undertake, we are most likely to achieve success and victory.

On hearing about the victory of Rama's army on the first day, Ravan, agitated and eager to fight entered the battlefield with his army. Rama completely disarmed Ravan, as well as dismounted his chariot. Consequently, Ravan, shaken, humiliated and unarmed returned to his palace alone on foot. Now being aware and able to gauge the strength of Rama, the demon king became scared of his actions to declare war against the Lord. Thus, Ravan instructed his men to awaken the mighty and gigantic Kumbhakarna.

Kumbhakarna was the younger brother of Ravan, but he was older than Vibhishan. Kumbhakarna was granted his boon as asked of Lord Brahma to eat for 6 months, and then sleep for the remaining 6 months of the year. Hence, many attempts were made to awaken him, such as poking him, and playing loud musical instruments, but all failed miserably. Finally, a lot of food was brought to him, and with that strong, delightful aroma of food that filled the air, the gigantic Kumbhakarna was awakened. After having his fill, he inquired about the reason for waking him prematurely, and was then referred to the King, Ravan.

Ravan then narrated everything that transpired to his brother, but unlike Ravan, Kumbhakarna saw the grave mistake that Ravan committed by abducting Sita. He also tried to convince Ravan to return Sita as Rama is the Lord of the Universe, but Ravan scolded him. Kumbhakarna realized his death and Ravan's destruction was inevitable as there is none who can withstand Rama's prowess and striking arrows. Nonethelesss, Kumbhakarna saw it befitting to support his brother Ravan in his hour of need.

While it is only right to stand by a relative or friend in their times of need or distress, it does not mean that we have to support their wrongdoings. Instead, we can help them if possible to get out of a difficult situation, but not at the cost of endangering our safety and well-being or sacrificing our lives. Actions have consequences, and one must be prepared to accept and deal with the results of his/her bad choices or evil actions.

As gigantic Kumbhakarna entered the battlefield, Vibhishan tried to convince his brother to retreat and surrender at the feet of Rama. However, Kumbhakarna maintained that he must stand by his elder brother, Ravan. His gigantic form and outrage struck terror among Rama's army, as he easily crushed many of the apes. Thus, to prevent the army from becoming disheartened, Rama took up the challenge against Kumbhakarna and slayed him to the delight of his army. Conversely, Ravan grieved over his brother's death and was consoled by his three sons, Atikaya, Narantak and Devantak who then entered the battlefield and met with the same fate as Kumbhakarna.

At this juncture, Atikaya's mother, another wife of Ravan, lamented over her son's death. She verbally abused Ravan for being the root cause for the loss of so many innocent lives which will bring about the ultimate ruin of Lanka. A shaken Ravan was now comforted by his most influential son, Indrajeet who then entered the battlefield.

A fierce battle then ensued through which Indarjeet bound Rama and Lakshman helpless with serpent darts. Hence, both Rama and Lakshman fell unconscious on the ground.

Indrajeet returned to the palace and proudly embraced his father sharing the good news. They both rejoiced at what they thought was now a sure sign of victory for them. In contrast, Sita hearing the terrible news was overwhelmed with grief. Likewise, Sugriv and the Army became worried, but the wise, thoughtful Hanuman always found a way out of every difficulty or challenging situation that unfolded. Thus, Hanuman brought the golden eagle, Garud who quickly released Rama and Lakshman from the serpent darts. Immediately, they both sat up strong, and determined to continue the battle.

The following day, a fierce battle was fought between Indrajeet and Lakshman. Realizing that it was difficult to defeat Indarjeet as he resorted to cunning means by making himself invisible at times, Lakshman asked permission of Rama to use the *Shakti Spear* to defeat Indarjeet. However, Rama disapproved of Lakshman's idea as he explained that it would be unethical to use that weapon at that particular time. However, the cunning Indrajeet struck Lakshman with the powerful *Shakti Ban*, and Lakshman fell unconscious on the ground. The mighty Hanuman instantly lifted Lakshman and carried him to safer grounds.

That was another proud moment for Indrajeet and Ravan as they celebrated their victory. In contrast, grief-stricken Rama placed his beloved brother on his lap as he sadly recollected fond memories of Lakshman always being by his side. Rama vowed to give up his own life if Lakshman does not survive the attack that has befallen him. Everyone present felt the distress of Lord Rama and thus, assessing the situation, Hanuman took leave to find a physician.

Hanuman requested Sushen, the physician of Ravan to come to the aid of Lakshman, but Royal protocol bounded him. As such, Sushen feared for his own life and dared not venture out to save the enemy. While Hanuman understood his position, it was an emergency to save the life of another human being, moreso, someone near and dear to Hanuman.

With no time to be wasted, Hanuman lifted Sushen's hut with him intact and flew to Rama's Camp. Sushen was reluctant to act, but being reminded of his first and foremost duty as a doctor to save lives, Sushen attended to the wounded Lakshman. He then advised that the Sanjeevani herb is fetched before dawn to cure the terrible wound that Lakshman sustained, as that was his only chance of survival. The Sanjeevani herb grew on the Himalayas very far away. Thus, it was impossible for someone to fetch it overnight.

Hence, again it was only the mighty, powerful Hanuman who could have successfully perform that task. Thus, Hanuman took flight on his journey with the gracious Lord Rama deeply enshrined in his heart. Having been informed of this task through his spies, Ravan sent Kalnemi, a master of sorcery to halt Hanuman on his way. Some distance away, in a most beautiful ashram close to a flowing stream, sat Kalnemi in the disguise of a Sage absorbed in devotion chanting *'Ram Naam'*. Seeing thus, Hanuman descended to pay his respects to what he perceived to be a devotee of his Lord Rama.

Kalnemi sent Hanuman for a refreshing bath in the flowing stream. As Hanuman entered the water, his foot was bitten by a crocodile, but Hanuman was not the least bit hurt as his body was tough like steel. Nonetheless, Hanuman grabbed the crocodile by its mouth and easily ripped it apart. The crocodile succumbed to its injury, thereafter adopting her original divine form as she was cursed by a Sage. She then informed Hanuman that the fake Saint is a demon,

Kalnemi. Hanuman returned from his bath and destroyed Kalnemi then rushed ahead on his mission.

On reaching the Himalayas, Hanuman was unable to identify the Sanjevani herb. Thus, with no time to waste, He lifted the peak of the Dronagiri Mountain, where the medical herbs grew and took flight on his return journey. As Hanuman flew over Ayodhya, he was spotted by Bharat who thought Hanuman was a demon and struck him down. Hanuman fell on the ground and in his semi-conscious state, he chanted '*Ram, Ram, Ram*'.

Bharat realized his mistake, then inquired from Hanuman of his identity and purpose. Hanuman narrated it all to Bharat who was grief-stricken over the agony of his beloved brothers and *bhabi* in Lanka. Bharat mounted Hanuman on a high speed-arrow to help compensate for the time lost, so that Hanuman could have arrived before sunrise to save Lakshman's life.

Indeed, the mighty, powerful, never-failing Hanuman arrived at his destination before sunrise, and Lakshman's wound treated with the Sanjeevani herb. Lakshman aroused fully energetic and was ready to rush towards the battlefield to resume the battle with Indarjeet. Meanwhile, Indarjeet started a "special yagna" (prayer ceremony) in the temple of *Nikumbhila* (deity of the demons) to become invincible. Lakshman, having been informed of this by Vibhishan hastened to the temple and provoked Indarjeet, thus interrupting his Yagna.

A fierce battle ensued between Lakshman and Indarjeet. Indarjeet now recognizing his inevitable demise by Lakshman's prowess, fled the scene to meet with his family one last time. He then sadly took leave of his wife and parents and returned like a true warrior to the battlefield. Through a fierce battle with Lakshman, Indarjeet was killed. Ravan was devastated as the news reached him as never before had Indarjeet been defeated in battle. Now devoid of all his powerful warriors, Ravan left with no other option, had to prepare for the battlefield.

As the war reached its climax with the fiercest of all battles between Rama and Ravan, Rishi Agastya gives *'Aditya Mantra'* or sacred mantra to Rama. On the other hand, Ravan addresses his army for the last time. The battle began between Rama and Ravan - 2 most powerful warriors, one on the path of righteousness and the other on the path of unrighteousness respectively. Rama's never failing arrows struck the mighty Ravan, and he fell unconscious. His Charioteer then quickly drove away, taking Ravan out of danger. After regaining consciousness, Ravan returned to the battlefield, and the battle continued until sunset.

It was the last night of the war, and both Mandodari and Sita were greatly agitated as it became inevitable that one of them would be widowed. Hence, Mandodari pleaded with her husband for the last time to surrender to Rama, but Ravan refused to retreat. He boldly entered his prayer room and delivered a strong outburst to *Mahakaal* (Lord Shiva). When one engages in evil deeds, one must not expect support from God, families and friends. One must be mindful, that an individual is solely responsible for their actions and choices in life. Thus, one must take full responsibility for it and not blame God or anyone when things go wrong.

As Ravan walked towards the entrance on his way out, Mandodari being so terrified performed her husband's pooja for what she feared might be the last time of seeing him alive. Simultaneously, Sita implored *Goddess Bhavani* to protect her husband and brother-in-law as the war reached its climax. Similarly, Rama and Lakshman offered prayer to their family Deity, Lord Surya at dawn, as they sought blessings to add glory to the *Raghukul Dynasty*, whether victory or defeat as Destiny decreed.

Rama's victory & reunion with Sita

Ravan entered the battlefield on his chariot armed with many powerful weapons, while Rama stood barefeet on the ground armed with only his bow and arrows. Seeing thus, the Devatas in the Heavens felt it was a grave injustice to Sri Rama. Thus, Indra sent his chariot to support Rama, but he hesitated to accept it as he was capable of achieving his task/purpose independent of others. After deliberation, Rama accepted the chariot and a fierce, decisive battle took place between Rama and Ravan. Like his son Indrajeet, the vile demon Ravan employed cunning means to defeat Rama, but the noble Rama honored ethical codes throughout his battles and that of his army.

Ravan was very powerful and had conquered many great warriors in battle, but he certainly was no match for Rama's prowess. As Rama's arrows cut off his head, another head instantly grew. Rama in a state of confusion looked at Vibhishan who then advised Rama that the 10-headed Ravan can only be slain by drying up the nectar in his navel. That was the boon that he received from Lord Brahma when he (Ravan) asked for immortality.

Rama then used the *Brahmastra* which pierced Ravan's navel. In shock with wide-opened eyes, Ravan instantly recognized Rama as the Lord of the Universe and chanted Rama's name as he fell unto the ground. Thus, Ravan was killed, and Rama and his army were victorious in the war. Malayavan, Mandodari and other relatives of Ravan rushed to the battlefield on hearing the terrible news. They all, including Vibhishan, grieved Ravan's death as expected. Noone can mentally nor emotionally prepare oneself for the loss of a loved one, although in some cases that may be the expectation. Rama also bowed to the departed soul of Ravan as he was a mighty warrior and moreso, of the Brahmin caste.

It was on Vijaya Dashami or Dussehra, which is the tenth day after the auspicious nine day celebration of *Navraatri*, in the month of Ashvin (September-October), that Ravan was killed. Navraatri is a nine (9) day/night period dedicated to the worship of the Universal Mother, *Maha Shakti Durga Maata* in her nine manisfestations. Preceding Ravan's demise, Rama had devoutly worshipped Maha Shakti Durga Maata during the 9-day period. As such, Durga Maata was pleased with Rama's steadfast devotion and blessed him with victory.

Similarly, as stated in *Devi Puraan,* it was also on Vijaya Dashami or Dussehra that the Universal Mother, *Durga Maata* killed the mighty demon, Mahishasur. Mahishasur secured a strange boon from the Creator, *Lord Brahma* that every drop of his blood that fell on the Earth will bring forth another demon as potent as him. Thus, Maha Shakti Durga adopted the form of *Kaali Maata* and collected his blood in a bowl, thus preventing it from dropping on the Earth. In that way, Maha Shakti Durga Maata killed that mighty demon and restored peace and happiness in the world.

Back in Lanka, Hanuman was sent by Rama to deliver the good news of their victory to Sita. Hanuman was delighted to meet with the Mother of the Universe once again. Finding Sita at peace deeply absorbed in her thoughts, Hanuman approached her with the good news. Sita was delighted to see Hanuman, and he gladly narrated everything to her. Sita stood motionless as the long-awaited good news left her totally spellbound. Sometimes amidst our anxiety and sufferings we prayer devoutly for a long time for relief, so when it finally happened, we are unable to react at that moment in time.

After the last rites of Ravan was performed, Rama sent Lakshman to complete the coronation of Vibhishan as the New King of Lanka. Vibhishan visited Rama's camp to receive his divine guidance and blessings. Rama advised Vibhishan to follow the code of ethics and righteous conduct as Monarch and also to worship the Deity of the demons. Visbhishan then took leave of Rama to make preparations for Sita to be reunited with Rama with all honors. Lakshman grew impatient for the reunion of Rama and Sita as he felt the immense pain and suffering of his *bhabi* being separated from Rama. Rama then cautioned Lakshman that "*one must not act in haste as it may likely lead to regret*".

As they all gathered to receive Sita who was brought in a beautifully decorated palanquin, the monkeys and bears were fighting to get a glimpse of Rama's most beautiful consort. Recognizing thus, Rama smiled and ordered the henchmen to place the palanquin down, so that Sita can walk towards him. In that way, everyone will have a chance to behold her Divine Form. As Sita approached Rama, he stopped her to the dismay of all and then instructed Lakshman to prepare the fire for Sita's '*agni-pariksha*' or fire test. Lakshman cried out and question his brother's motive as He maintained his *bhabi* is innocent. Rama affirmed that Lakshman followed his instructions without delay.

A grief-stricken Lakshman prepared the fire and Sita entered, thus retaining her Real Form from Agni Devata, which was not known to anyone present, but Sita and Rama. Hence, the pure and chaste Sita was unharmed by the fire and took her rightful place at the left side of her beloved Rama. The Devatas in the heavens showered flowers granting blessings on Rama's victory, as well as the reunion of Sita and Rama.

At that blissful, happy moment, Dasrath appeared in the Heavens and communicated to Rama how proud he felt of him. Dasrath told Rama to ask for a boon and he will grant it. Rama requested of his loving father to withdraw the curse he placed on Kaikeyi when he denounced her at Rama's departure to the forest. Dasrath smilingly and lovingly obliged as Rama's compassionate nature immensely pleased him. Dasrath blessed Rama abundantly along with Sita and Lakshman. In the life of a noble soul, there is always a reason why things happen, favorable or unfavorable to us that is sometimes known or unknown. Understanding thus, Rama maintained a pure mind and guileless heart, and thus never blamed anyone for his misfortune. Rama dealt with his adversity in a calm, dispassionate, moral and ethical way that befits a righteous soul.

Vibhishan promptly prepared the *Puskpak Viman* (flying chariot) to transport Rama, Sita, and Lakshman on their return to Ayodhya. Hanuman, Sugriv, and Vibhishan also accompanied them on their journey to witness Rama's Coronation. Rama desired to visit Rishi Bharadwaj's Ashram on his return journey, thus they halted. It was the final day in completion of the 14 years of exile. Remembering Bharat's vow to end his life if Rama was late by one day, Rama dispatched Hanuman to convey the good news to Bharat that he was on his way without any delay. Next, they halted again for Sita to pay respect to Ganga Maata as she promised on their return. At that place, Rama's friend Guha also joined them to witness Rama's Coronation.

The people of Ayodhya grew impatient as they awaited the return of their Lord Rama. On the contrary, Bharat prepared to end his life as it was the last day for the return of Rama and he had not yet received any news. Hence, Guru Vashistha offered good counsel to him that he should have faith in Rama who is true to his word. Vashistha also advised that *the Lord works in mysterious ways as one's misfortune can change into a good fortune at the last moment.* Thus, he advised Bharat not to take any harsh action, but to be patient until the very last moment. Advising thus, Hanuman arrived with the long-awaited, good news and delivered Bharat from his anxiety. Bharat felt delighted at heart that Rama had kept his word and was therefore, eager to behold his Divine form.

Rama's return to Ayodhya & his Coronation

The Queen Mothers, Guru, Shatrughna and the people of Ayodhya gathered with Bharat in Nandigram where Bharat resided for the 14 years. They looked about anxiously, then suddenly sighted the *Puspak Viman*. Alas! Rama arrived in Ayodhya to the delight of all, as tears of joy welled up in the eyes of his family and the people. As Rama, Sita, and Lakshman alighted from the chariot, they first paid their respects to Guru Vashistha, and after taking his blessings, they proceeded to the Queen Mothers.

It was a very emotional time for the Mothers to once again behold and embraced their beloved sons and daughter-in-law, as well as the union of all four Princes and Princesses. Bharat wiped the dust from Rama's feet with his shawl, and lovingly and gentle lifted Rama's feet and placed it unto his sandal which Bharat kept on the throne for 14 years. Tears of love and joy trickled down Bharat's cheeks as he could not contain his deep emotions of finally having his beloved family back together. High emotions filled the tranquil atmosphere as the Royal family and the people of Ayodhya reunited in love, unity, and happiness.

As preparations were underway for the long, overdued Coronation of Rama, he noticed Manthara's absence. Hence, upon inquiry from Kaikeyi, Rama was informed that Manthara was so remorseful for perverting Kaikeyi's mind that she had since then, locked herself in her room. The merciful Lord Rama called on Sita and Lakshman to accompany him as they proceeded to meet with Manthara.

As they entered the dark room, Rama called out to Manthara in the same manner that he addressed his Mothers. Manthara in disbelief, wept bitterly at Rama's loving disposition, reflecting on the way she taunted Rama, Sita, and Lakshman. Rama understood the guilt in her heart and with a beautiful smile on his lips, He reassured her that no one ought to be blamed. He assured Manthara that they do not harbor any ill-feelings towards her. Rama advised Sita and Lakshman to seek her blessings. Manthara who was filled with remorse could not control her flowing tears.

That fabulous day that the people of Ayodhya craved for had finally dawned after fourteen long years. The courtyard and palace were beautifully decorated beyond description, and the sound of musical instruments filled the air. Men and women alike sang enchanting, beautiful songs and danced in ecstasy and jubilation. Kings from the neighboring Kingdoms, as well as King Janak were invited to witness the Grand Event in Ayodhya. As Guru Vashistha along with other Brahmanas chanted the sacred mantras, Rama was anointed the King of Ayodhya and seated on his left side was his beloved consort, Sita who was now the Queen. The Royal Pair of Ram and Sita shone forth like the radiant brilliance of the Sun to the delight of the eyes and hearts of all present.

Gifts were distributed to the Guests when Sita indicated silently to Rama that she would like to present to Hanuman a special gift. That is, a token of gratitude for his support and help during her time of distress and suffering. She lovingly removed her pearl necklace which Rama gladly and affectionately presented to his beloved messenger, Hanuman. Hanuman thus, reluctantly accepted the necklace, however, to the bewilderment of all present, He broke the necklace and bit the beads as He closely examined it.

Rama inquired of Hanuman about the strange phenomenon, to which Hanuman replied that he is searching to see whether *Rama and Sita are present in the beads*. Hanuman further exclaimed that nothing was of value to him, if it does not contain Rama and Sita. Affirming thus, Hanuman tore open his chest and revealed to all, the presence of Rama and Sita in his heart. Everyone present were immensely touched by Hanuman's pure character, simplicity, humility, unconditional love and devotion towards Rama. Rama and Sita smiled lovingly and blessed Hanuman abundantly.

Hanuman, Ram & Sita

Fulfilling the command of his father Dasrath, Rama occupied the throne with the assistance of his beloved brothers and ministers. He ruled the Kingdom in all fairness and righteous conduct. Like his father's Rulership, the people of Ayodhya were contented and they lived happily. With the affairs of Ayodhya placed in capable hands and having thus achieved such great accomplishments, the Queen Mothers proceeded on a pilgrimage. Further, the Great Sage Valmiki received intuition, and at the behest of Lord Brahma he commenced writing the *Ramayan – the life story of Sri Rama.*

Previously, when Hanuman sought Garud's assistance and he saw the helpless state of Rama and Lakshman lying unconscious from the serpent spell placed by Indarjeet, Garud entertained doubt whether Rama was the Lord of the Universe. To clarify his doubts, Garud proceeded to Lord Brahma who referred him to Lord Shiva.

The Great Lord Shiva who continuously meditates on the lotus-like feet of Rama then advised Garud to listen to Ram Katha as narrated by Kakabhushundi to clarify his doubts. The golden eagle, Garuda then journey to the *Mansa Lake* on the mountains and sat among thousands of other birds in devotion. Garud listened attentively as the crow, Kakabhushundi devoutly narrated the glories and greatness of Sri Rama.

Similarly, the charming consort of Lord Shiva in her previous birth as Sati also doubted whether Rama was the Lord of the Universe after seeing him weeping and helplessly searching for his beloved wife, Sita in the forest. However, the Great Lord Shiva who knows and sees everything clearly through his third eye or divine vision, comprehended what was going on in Sati's mind. Thus, he tried to clarify Sati's doubts, but she was not convinced of his explanations and wanted to discover the truth. Lord Shiva permitted her to fulfil her desire and continued his meditation on the *lotus-like feet* of his Lord Rama.

As Rama and Lakshman wandered through the forest in search of Sita, Sati disguised herself as Sita and approached Rama. She did not believe her husband, Shiva and wanted to test Rama herself to determine if he was really the Lord of the Universe that's acting as an ordinary mortal. However, to her surprise, Rama immediately recognized her as the lovely consort of Lord Shiva. Rama prostrated before her and inquired about her wandering all alone in the forest without her Lord, Shiva.

Sati was bewildered and felt extremely embarrassed of her foolish action. However, the merciful Lord who understood her intentions, then cast his *Maya* (illusion) over her. Thus everywhere Sati looked she saw myriads of Sita and Rama in all directions. As Sati stood motionless in bewilderment before the Lord, she was overpowered by embarrassment and remorse and thus, fainted.

Sati was an incarnation of the Universal Mother, so we may ponder the reason for this demeaning action on her part. God teaches us through his own example about *cause and effect*. Moreover, an effective leader is one who *'walks the talk'* and not just lecture to others. This means, an influential leader is one who practices what he preaches to his people as ideally exemplified by Sri Rama.

After regaining consciousness, Sati returned to her Lord, Shiva. He sat comfortably under the shady banyan tree and had witnessed it all through his Divine sight, but Sati was ignorant of that. Lord Shiva then politely requested of Sati to relate to him her experience of meeting with Rama. Sati then stated that upon seeing Sri Rama, she did exactly as he (Shiva) had advised. That is, she prostrated herself before him and then returned, she claimed.

Lord Shiva uttered not a word and went into deep meditation as he vowed to renounce Sati as she was no longer worthy of being his consort. She firstly committed a grievous wrong by disguising herself as Sita, as she pretended to be the wife of another, and thus, insulted her husband's love and dignity. Moreover, rather than confess her wrongdoing and atone for her mistake, she lied about it to her enlighten husband who knew the truth of the matter.

To unknowingly commit a mistake is a pity that might be forgiven, but to knowingly commit a mistake and make matters worst by lying about it makes it more difficult to forget and forgive. Hence, in this scenario, this grievous wrong was unforgivable as posited by Lord Shiva in his mind. As the days passed by, Sati noticed that her husband became withdrawn from her and thus, realized that Lord Shiva knew the *truth of the matter.* With a deep sense of guilt and remorse for her wrongdoing, Sati prayed to Rama in her heart. She requested of the Lord to devise a plan for her to rid herself of that body, as being rejected by her husband, Lord Shiva, her life holds no more meaning and significance.

The all-merciful, compassionate Lord Rama who is ever favorably disposed to the downtrodden and to those who seek refuge in him endorsed Sati's request. In due time, one day Sati observed many aerial cars of different colors and types flying by and inquired of her husband about the strange phenomenon. Lord Shiva informed her that her father Daksha was hosting a Grand Yagna and those are the many guests traveling to his place.

Sati was struck with disbelief that her father did not invite her for such a grand celebration. Nonetheless, being a close relative, she requested of her husband to attend. Lord Shiva then explained to her that it was not wise to attend as they were not invited. Although one needs no formal invitation to visit one's near and dear ones, it was a deliberate act to not invite them. In light of that, Lord Shiva suggested to Sati that it will not be wise to attend.

However, Sati insisted on going to her father's place despite the many ways her husband tried to deter her. Lord Shiva tried to make her see reasons to not attend, yet she was not convinced. Finally, Lord Shiva permitted her to fulfil her burning desire. The moment Sati arrived at her father's place, she was treated with scorn as no one welcomed her for fear of Daksha. She instantly realized that her husband was right, but it was too late. Moreover, she became annoyed when she observed that no offerings were made to her husband, the Great Lord Shiva.

Her heart was overcome with grief as she was unable to tolerate the grievous insult done to her Lord, and moreso the fact that she did not pay heed to her husband's sound advice once again. Through her vulnerable state of mind to redeem herself of her wrongdoings, as well as the pity of being an offspring of Daksha, as she thought, Sati jumped into the Sacrificial fire and ended her life. In due time, she was reborn as Parvati and had to undergo austere penance to again have Lord Shiva as her husband.

Back in Ayodhya after some time, one day a *dooby's* (washerman) wife went across the river by boat to visit her mother. On her way back the riverbanks were flooded due to torrential rain. As a result, the boatman was unable to set sail; thus with no other means to cross the river, she was forced to overnight at the boatman's hut. In the morning, the water subsided, and the boatman was then able to ferry her across the river. Upon reaching home, the *dooby* accused his wife of infidelity and threw her out of the house. Moreover, the *dooby* (washerman) drew reference to Rama. He exclaimed that he is not like Rama to accept his wife after she stayed at Ravan's place for many days.

Unfortunately, the *dooby's* accusations on his wife instigated the people of Ayodhya to entertain doubts about their Queen, Sita's purity and character. Moreso, the *dooby's* homeless wife in deep distress went to the palace to seek justice from the King, Rama but sadly, was turned away by the guards as the King, Rama was asleep. Rama was annoyed with his guards when he learned about the woman's visit to meet with him, but turned away. Rama stressed that no one should come to his door and return empty-handed. In order words, He pledged that every person would receive justice under his Rulership. Rama instructed his guards to search for the woman, but unfortunately they were unable to find her.

After some time, Rama was informed by his Secretary that people were daily engaging in negative discussions about the Queen, Sita. Hence, in disguise Rama went out to the villages and mingled with the people. He was shocked and deeply hurt to hear the inferences and false opinions of some people as they talked unseemly things about Sita, despite the many sacrifices and trials she endured.

Upon his return to the palace as days passed by, Sita noticed that her husband was withdrawn and having inquired about the reason for his sadden state, he remained silent. His disturbed state of mind knew no measure as He expressed his innermost feelings to Lord Shiva, praying for divine guidance and peace of mind. King Rama was placed in such a difficult situation having to choose between his beloved, innocent wife and his subjects, the people of Ayodhya.

Soon, Rama's brothers observed his alarming appearance, thus they approached Sita for answers. At that particular time, Rama, looking quite depressed walked in after a long day at the Royal Court. He refused to partake of the food that was served to him claiming that he was not hungry. Rama's behavior confirmed their suspicions as Sita and his brothers knew something was definitely amiss. Having inquired of Rama about the reason for his worry, Rama smilingly responded that he just feels tired. He added that he felt to retire to the forest with Sita to undergo *tapasya* (penance). Further, he stated that since Bharat already had the experience, he felt confident that Bharat will do well as his successor (Sargar).

Sadly, the brothers reacted negatively to Rama's reply as Bharat, Lakshman, and Shatrughna became very emotional and blamed themselves. They expressed their thoughts that perhaps they had fallen short in their service to King Rama, and thus the reason he wants to leave. Sita also was in profound shock to hear Rama's reply. After Rama closely observed his loving brothers sensitive and emotional reactions to his proposal, he lovingly claimed that it was just a joke. Thus, Rama realized that leaving with Sita was not an option for him (Sargar).

The next morning Sita sent one of her trusted maids to go out and mingle with the people to find out about their conversations. She warned that her maid took extra caution so that noone recognizes her. Sita was terribly hurt when her maid related to her what the people were saying about her (Sita). The maid provided a full report that people claimed that Sita was a stigma to the Throne and that she was the weakness of the King, and other unseemly accusations.

Later in the afternoon, a very disturbed Lakshman came to find out the *truth of the matter* from his *bhabi*, Sita. She assured him that none of the brothers were at fault, but just then Rama arrived. Knowing the truth of the matter and observing the strong bond of both brothers, Sita mentally affirmed her next course of action. It was the only solution to restore peace and happiness among the people of Ayodhya (Sargar).

Rama renounces Sita

Sita silently communicated her thoughts at the feet of Goddess Bhavani and prayed for strength and courage to act on her decision if it was indeed right. As she meditated on the beautiful form of the Goddess, a flower fell off Bhavani's hands onto Sita's palms. Sita felted delighted to once again secure the blessings of the Goddess Mother, as she interpreted that as a sign that her decision is indeed right (Sargar).

Sita realized that Rama, out of deep love for her was placed in such a helpless situation, whereby he had to choose to stand by her or the people of Ayodhya. Thus, due to Rama's hesitancy to take such a tough decision, she chose to act and do what was right to the best interest of the people, although it may cause her much pain and separation from the love of her life, Rama.

When Rama returned from the Court, Sita observed his worried, restless state and thus, addressed him in polite, but firm tones. She communicated to him that she knew the cause of his worry which is her. Rama was shocked that she knew the truth as he avoided telling her of the mean accusations on her by the people. She questioned why Rama could not tell her about it, but Rama maintained such indecent claims were not worth sharing with her.

Sita reminded Rama of his oath upon being crowned King, that he will serve the people first, above all else including his own family. Moreover, she firmly reminded him that he had sworn to carry out the "will" of the people so they can always be happy and contented, regardless of his personal feelings. Sita offered wise counsel to her beloved husband that there was no other way out of that dreadful situation, but to favor and honor the people's "will and mandate". Rama hesitated, but finally conceded as Sita made him see the reason from all angles of Royal etiquette.

Lakshman was summoned to take Sita to the forest and leave her there. Lakshman questioned Rama's decision as he maintained once again that Sita was innocent, but Rama instructed him to go forth. After being forced to take such a cruel decision, it hurts more when questioned about it. Thus, Rama refused to have any further discussions with anyone about that deeply emotional matter.

Sita mounted the chariot dressed in the garb of a hermit once again, with an aching heart and tearful eyes she gazed at her Lord, as a devastated Lakshman was forced to drive the chariot. Rama, so heartbroken through separation from his beloved Sita again, stood lost in thoughts of his beloved wife. As the dust of the wheels of the chariot filled the air, Rama with teary eyes, stood motionless as if his soul had left his body.

As Lakshman reached the forest, Sita disembarked and just walked away. A grief-stricken Lakshman placed the dust of her feet on his forehead. As Sita's feet touched the ground, the Great Sage Valmiki felt her presence (the Universal Mother). He set forth to meet with her. Sita walked deeper into the forest and suddenly came into contact with the wise and learned Sage Valmiki. He appeared as though he was waiting for her. Thus, she was not abandoned in the forest to suffer in distress as she immediately received support.

Sita expressed her grief to Valmiki as she broke down in tears. She requested that Valmiki kept her identity hidden as she no longer wanted to be addressed as Sita. She also offered her unborn child as a disciple of the learned Sage and requested of him that her child remained ignorant of his father's identity. She proclaimed that a self-made and independent man does his parents proud. Sita's humility and purity significantly touched an ascetic as Valmiki, and thus He offered her shelter. He assured her that the people of Ayodhya would one day repent for their sins (Sargar).

In the absence of family and especially in times of need, one may confide in someone that one feels close to as a relative or friend and thus, share one's innermost feelings and secrets. Fortunately, the vulnerable Sita met with a genuinely "holy man" who was the most appropriate and trusted person to express her innermost feelings. Moreover, he thoroughly understood her helpless situation and offered support. In real life, one must be careful of the person one chooses to confide in and to trust. However, if that person donot respect and appreciate you, then such a person may take advantage of your vulnerability and will betray your trust or harm you.

As Sita approached Valmiki's Ashram, all the disciples, both young and old, were fascinated by her incomparable beauty and radiance. As her name was withheld and she was found in the forest, they named her Vandevi, *the Goddess of the Forest*. Valmiki entrusted her in the loving care of Gautami Maa, who was the oldest disciple. He also advised that she took extra care of Sita as she was pregnant. Two teenage girls were also assigned to watch over Sita and keep her company. Sita was escorted to one of the nearby ashrams. A kush-grass mat was then laid on the ground where she retired to rest (Sargar).

Upon Lakshman's return to the palace, King Rama instructed him to prepare a kush-grass bed on the floor for him. Lakshman felt the pain of his beloved brother, but reluctantly carried out his orders. In that way, although Rama remained in the Palace as the King, he gave up all Royal comforts, treats and pleasures and thus, subjected himself to the same living conditions as his dearly beloved wife, Sita. Daily, he fulfilled his duty as the King in the Royal Court, but afterwards, he was completely absorbed in thoughts of his beloved Sita. Rama became so quiet and withdrawn that Lakshman could not bear his brother's silent suffering anymore. Thus, he secretly reached out to King Janak to come to Rama's aid.

Rama was shocked to see Sita's father, Janak at the entrance to the palace. A grief-stricken Lakshman then revealed to his brother that he summoned King Janak. King Rama lovingly greeted his father-in-law and invited him inside. King Janak was also saddened over his daughter's banishment, but when he saw the kush-grass bed on the floor, he was more saddened that Rama's suffering was more than that of his daughter, Sita. Janak consoled Rama and stressed that he was proud of his daughter for the decision she had made to uphold her duty and dharma (religious & cultural practices).

Janak presented a letter to Rama that Sita had sent to him on the night before she left. Sita explained to her father that he should not blame her husband, Rama for her banishment, nor should he visit Rama as he may not be in any position to face him (Janak). Janak also informed Rama that Sita's mother had fallen very ill on hearing the sad news. Rama, immediately ignoring his own grief, requested of King Janak to accompany him to visit Sita's mother. Rama was permitted by his Guru Vashistha to take leave and thus, Janak gladly took Rama and Lakshman to Mithila. Sita's mother, Sunaina was glad at heart to see Rama, but sadly expressed her regret that Sita was not with him. Janak, a storehouse of virtue then imparted spiritual advice to Rama (Sargar).

For many days, a depressed Sita was deeply engrossed in thoughts of her beloved husband, Rama. Seeing thus, Valmiki advised that her grieving state of mind was not healthy for her baby. He added that her deep sorrow would also reach and affect her husband as *two loving hearts beat in consonance with each other*. Moreover, he reminded her of the reason why she left Ayodhya and suggested that she should not let her sacrifice go in vain. Lastly, he advised that she focused her mind on good and positive thoughts for the health and well-being of all concerned, her baby, husband and herself. With those powerful words of wisdom and enlightenment,

Sita felt relieved of her deep distress and expressed her gratitude to the learned and wise Sage Valmiki.

After Valmiki's wise counsel, Sita then broke her silence and started socializing with her fellow disciples. Moreover, her beautiful smile returned as she began to accept her *new life* in companion with the Holy Sages and noble disciples, despite being separated from her Lord, Sri Rama. She daily helped Gautami Maa grind the grains, prepare the vegetables and the food. Gautami Maa would lovingly feed Sita and shower her with love and affection as a daughter.

Further, Sita would daily listen to the recital of the religious text as imparted by the Great Sage Valmiki. This is believed to be quite appropriate and beneficial for the safety, health and general well-being of the developing fetus in the mother's womb. Moreover, it is believed that an unborn baby in the mother's womb is likely to develop qualities of the mother. Hence, it is highly recommended that pregnant women entertain pure thoughts, and engage in good, noble actions, and righteous conduct as a means to help bring forth good offspring.

Back in Ayodhya, Sage Chyavan visited King Rama seeking his help to save the Brahmanas and the people of Mathura from the demon King Lavnasur. Like the demon King Kans, the maternal uncle of Sri Krishna who was eventually killed by Sri Krishna, the mighty and powerful demon, Lavnasur was also creating havoc among the people of Mathura. He interrupted the sacrifices of the Brahmanas for human welfare and killed many Holy men and innocent people.

Rama swore to protect Chyavan and the innocent people of Mathura. Rama assigned Shatrughna and presented him with a secret weapon to destroy Lavnasur and the demons. Rama advised Shatrughna to stop at Valmiki's ashram to seek the blessings of Sage Valmiki on his journey to Mathura. Shatrughna bowed reverently to his brother and departed with the army.

Birth of Luv and Kush

Just as instructed by his brother Rama, Shatrughna arrived at the ashram of Valmiki as the flag of the Solar (Sun) Dynasty flew high. As fate decreed, at that same time, Sita gave birth to twin boys. Shatrughna stayed at the ashram of Valmiki and was informed by the Sage of the birth of the baby boys whose identity were withheld. The wise Sage Valmiki further communicated to Shatrughna that the boys are also of the *Solar Race* as him, so that makes him their Uncle. Valmiki thus added, in the absence of their father; the uncle can perform the *'Naam Sanskaar'* or naming ceremony of the babies and politely requested Shatrughna to fulfill that role.

Shatrughna was delighted to oblige and the boys were named, Luv and Kush. Shatrughna blessed the babies and he presented them with his pearl necklaces that bore the Solar (Sun) symbol that is the mark of distinction of those belonging to the *Raghukul Dynasty*. Sita felt most delighted at heart that her youngest brother-in-law was present to perform the necessary *sanskar* (ritual) at the birth of her babies in the absence of their father. She was also happy to have a glimpse of her brother-in-law as Shatrughan set forth on his first task. Taking the blessings of Valmiki, Shatrughna departed on his onward journey to Mathura.

Lavnasur slayed many holy men and innocent people through his brutal atrocities. Having reached Mathura, Shatrughna met with Sage Chyavan who gladly received him. The sage related the unfortunate outcome of the past battle between Lavnasur and Mandhata, an ancestor of Shatrughna. Lavnasur possessed a never-failing Trishul that makes it impossible to defeat him in battle. Thus, he employed that weapon to kill Mandhata.

The wise Sage related that incident to Prince Shatrughna so he would not make the same mistake as Mandhata to attack Lavnasur while in possession of that never failing weapon. Consequently,

Chyavan advised Shatrughna to attack Lavnasur as he leaves for his early morning sport when he was not in possession of that fatal weapon.

Heeding Chyavan's sound advice, Shatrughna waited outside the gate of Lavnasur's Palace. Lavnasur after worshipping the Trishul as was his daily routine, left for his morning sport. As soon as his chariot emerged through the gate, Shatrughna challenged him to battle. Lavnasur stood totally in shock and disbelief as he never expected such a challenge, and worst yet, was unable to turn back to retrieve his invincible Trishul.

Nonetheless, a fierce battle followed between Shatrughna and Lavnasur that claimed the life of that terrible demon, Lavnasur. Subsequently, Shatrughna was anointed the new King of Mathura. The people and Holy men rejoiced in ecstasy as they welcome their new King, who was a noble and righteous person. Rama and the people of Ayodhya on hearing the great news also celebrated Shatrughna's first victory as they lit festive lamps. Likewise, Sita though devoid of all Royal comforts, also lit a lamp to celebrate Shatrughna's victory (Sargar).

Sita sang beautiful lullabies as she rocked her babies to sleep. In due time, Sita sat in consultation with Valmiki. They discussed the benefits of Astrology, as planning and preparation were underway for the commencement of Luv and Kush's education. Even as toddlers, Sita taught her children about caring and sharing with each other. She also showed them how to help and pacify each other if one gets hurt, while also involving them in daily chores as she grounded the grains. In that way, Sita taught the world to teach children (both boys and girls) from a tender age to be kind, helpful and responsible so that they grow up being good human beings.

Back in Ayodhya, Rama was invited to witness the ascent of the Great Sage Agastya from his underwater penance after 12 years.

Sage Agastya was happy to meet with Rama and Lakshman and bestowed blessings on them. On the other side, Luv and Kush were growing up quickly, and they were the delight of the hearts of all, including the ascetic Valmiki who felt much love and attachment towards them. The boys were of age now to begin their education that included lessons in Vedanta, Physical Labor, and Meditation. Hence, the *Yagyopavit Ceremony* took place on a most auspicious day, thereby commencing the education of the young boys.

Sage Valmiki also taught the young boys Archery skills and Music. Thus, Luv and Kush sang Ramayan Katha to the amazement of their Guru, Valmiki who taught them about Rama's Katha. They were not aware that the Great King, Rama was their father as they were never informed by their mother of their father's name. Given their situation of separation from Rama, Sita deliberately withheld their father's identity as she thought the boys were too innocent to understand. Moreover, the given situation and time was not right to divulge that information as Sita wanted her sons to be self-made, young men who will not dwell on their father's wealth and prestige for recognition, but whom will independently develop their own noble identity.

Even at the tender age of five as Luv and Kush sang about Rama's Katha, the young boys recognized the cruel injustice done to Sita, while being ignorant of the fact that Sita was indeed their mother. Their young minds were disturbed over Sita's ongoing distress and sufferings as she was tested unfairly repeatedly. Thus, Luv reacts to the injustice done to her. They seek answers from their Guru and Mother, but they were told that they would know everything at the right time.

Sita complemented Valmiki's teaching with her home schooling, as she taught her sons about love and respect for others, not only humans, but plants and animals as well. She taught them about duty and responsibility as she took them along to help gather the fire sticks, fetch water from the lake and to feed the cows. In that way, she instilled in them moral values and ethical conduct, so that they can maintain the high standards set by the *Raghukul Dynasty* and thus, serve the people well.

In Ayodhya, Rama decided to perform *Ashwamedh Yagna*. Thus, Lakshman was instructed by Rama to undertake the necessary preparations. As Guru Vashistha and other Brahmanas gather in consultation of proper performance of the Yagna, it was proposed that Rama should remarry. That suggestion met with Rama's harsh disapproval, but the Holy men maintained that it was necessary for Rama to have his consort at his side to perform that particular Yagna.

They added that since Sita is not with him, then he must remarry to fulfil the conditions of undertaking such a sacred ritual. Rama argued that his beloved wife Sita was innocent and as such refused to even think of a second marriage. Rama suggested that the Gurus find some other way or means for the performance of the Yagna, as the idea of remarrying was not an option for him. When a truthful and righteous man is firm in his resolve to maintain his loyalty to his beloved wife, no negative influence, temptation or anyone's advice can convince him to break his oath. Another important point to be noted here is that there is no "one way" of doing things as one needs to explore the options for alternative methods or measures to righteously and adequately serve the purpose.

Meanwhile, Gautami Maa informed Sita about what was happening in Ayodhya. When Sita heard about the performance of the Yagna, she felt delighted, but when she heard about the proposal for the second marriage of Rama, she was devastated. That terrible news pierced her heart like a dagger, as she could not bear the thought of her beloved Lord, Rama remarrying in spite of knowing that she was innocent.

Sometimes the mere thought of something awful befalling us, a loved one or losing something we cherish, bring tears to our eyes and makes our heart tremble in fear. Hence, the more reason to develop a strong relationship with God and trust that our Master holds our best interest at heart and knows more than us what is best for us. Moreover, it is only God that truly understands our innermost feelings, challenges and problems, and will stand by us day and night, in good times and bad times throughout our life's journey and beyond.

There was a beautiful small temple of Maha Vishnu Bhagwan in the vicinity of the ashram whereby Sita performed her daily worship. In a state of shock and grief, she stood silently before the Lord as she recollected Rama's vow to her on their wedding night. Rama had declared to Sita that she would be the only woman in his life, even though it was the norm for Kings to have more than one wife. This Rama affirmed as his given word to her. Thus, heartbroken with tearful eyes, Sita offered her silent prayer to Maha Vishnu Bhagwan.

The next morning, Sita was pleased to hear about Rama's refusal to remarry. She felt delighted at heart that her beloved husband had kept his word and honored the oath, He made to her. At the same time, she repented having entertained doubts in her mind about her husband's loyalty towards her. She communicated that feeling of remorse to Valmiki who advised her to perform a specific ritual as atonement.

Valmiki, through his mysterious powers presented to Luv and Kush divine weapons. Luv and Kush once again inquired of their mother about the identity of their father. Sita then instructed them to fetch some lotus flower for her to perform a particular ritual and after that, she will reveal their father's identity. Anxiously, the boys took leave to gather the lotus flower from the lake.

Knowing Rama to always be firm in his resolve, Guru Vashistha in consultation with other Brahmanas proposed the idea of creating a golden statue of Sita. This *murti* will then be placed at Rama's side in the performance of the Yagna. The beloved Lord Rama readily approved of that brilliant idea. Thus, the necessary preparations were undertaken and the Ashwamedh Yagna was performed.

Prince Shatrughna then left for world conquest with the beautifully decorated, sacred horse. On seeing the horse as it passed by, other rulers and countrymen bowed in respect to it as they read the sign on the horse, as no one wanted to incur Rama's enmity. Inscribed in gold letters that was posted on the face of the horse read, *"the horse belonged to Rama, the King of Ayodhya and anyone who ceases the horse will have to do battle with the King, Rama"* (Tulsidass & Sargar).

On his return to Ayodhya, Shatrughna decided to rest for awhile at the outskirts of the city, and thus released the horse to graze. The horse wandered out of sight whereby, seeing the horse and reading the words, Luv and Kush accepted the challenge, and thus captured the sacred horse. Shatrughna and his men searched for the horse which was found in the captivity of Luv and Kush. They politely requested the boys to release the horse.

Luv and Kush meeting with Rama

Surprisingly, Luv and Kush refused to release the horse declaring that they accept the challenge. Shatrughna tried to convince the boys that the horse is not a toy as he perceived them to be ordinary little boys. However, since the boys insisted on engaging in battle, Shatrughna could no longer decline and so the battle began with Luv and Kush against their uncle. Strangely, Shatrughna and his army were defeated by Luv and Kush.

As the news reached Ayodhya, Rama sent Lakshman to retrieve the horse. Upon seeing the two charming, young boys, Lakshman could not believe that they possess such prowess to defeat his brother. Like Shatrughna, he also tried to convince the boys to retreat and release the horse, but to no avail. Thus, a fierce battle ensued, and Lakshman was also defeated in the battle.

Upon hearing the shocking, unbelievable news, Rama sent Bharat, Sugriv and the mighty Hanuman to retrieve the sacred horse. Bharat and Sugriv looked in bewilderment at the innocence of Luv and Kush, thus thinking whether those mere young boys possessed such valor. The wise Hanuman took a different approach and tried to inquire about the identity of Luv and Kush, but the boys' did not know their father nor did they know that their mother was Sita.

Hanuman closed his eyes, then affirmed silently, *"if my devotion is true to Rama, may the merciful Lord reveal to me the parents of the boys"* (Sargar). Instantly, Hanuman saw the beautiful form of Rama and Sita through his mind's eye. Gratefully, Hanuman was delighted to behold the offspring of his Master and thus, allowed himself to be bound by Luv and Kush. Hanuman was happy to be in the company of Luv and Kush, as he perceived them as his little Masters, and they also treated him affectionately. As Luv and Kush continued in battle, Bharat and Sugriv were also wounded and defeated.

Finally, came the Master himself, Rama, who was shocked beyond measure to behold the two young boys that captured the horse, and defeated his powerful brothers and the army of Ayodhya. Just as his brothers, Rama tried to persuade the delicate boys to give up their stubbornness and release the horse, but Luv and Kush showed no sign of retreating from battle. As much as Rama tried to deter the boys, they were determined to fight.

Moreover, Luv and Kush spoke bitterly to Rama and challenged his resolve to do justice to his lineage. Hence, Rama was left with no other option, but agreed to fight as returning without the horse would have been disgraceful to his rulership and lineage. As Rama mounted an arrow to his bow, and as Luv and Kush did likewise, the Great Sage Valmiki appeared before the boys and stopped the attempted battle.

Rama was shocked to see the Great Sage and stepped down from his chariot to pay his respect to Valmiki. Valmiki reminded Rama that protecting women and children is the duty of the King, so he should never consider doing battle with children. Rama explained that the boys were adamant to fight.

Valmiki turned to Luv and Kush and stated that it was not right of them to capture the sacred horse. Luv and Kush explained to their Guru Valmiki that they held the horse for two reasons. Firstly, as *Kshatriyas*, they were duty-bound to accept the challenge and secondly, Luv had some questions for Rama. Hence, they captured the horse as a means to enable Luv to meet with the King.

Both Sage Valmiki and King Rama were impressed of the wisdom and the courage of the young boys. Then, Luv ask Rama why did he renounce his wife Sita when he knew she was innocent. Rama, explained in detail that it is the first and foremost duty of a King to carry out the "will" of his people, regardless of whether it brings joy or sorrow to him. Hence, in honoring the high ideals set by his lineage, to please the people of Ayodhya, and to restore happiness among them, he was forced to renounce his beloved Sita.

On the contrary, Rama further explained that the *prime duty* of a common man is to take care of his immediate and extended family. Rama expressed to Luv and Kush how proud He was of their intelligence, courage and bravery. He advised them to seek their parents' permission when their education was over to visit the Royal Family in Ayodhya. Valmiki asked Hanuman to return with the sacred horse. The wise Hanuman confirmed with the Sage Valmiki that Luv and Kush are indeed the sons of Sita and Rama.

Luv and Kush returned home and presented the basket of lotuses to their loving mother Sita, to perform her specific ritual. Then they narrated at length to their mother all that had transpired that day and how they defeated the entire army of Ayodhya. Sita stood in shock and lamented over the grievous wrong her children had committed by engaging in battle with their relatives.

Luv and Kush were also shocked to hear that Rama was their father and the unfortunate Sita that they learned about was their mother. This was immediately confirmed by Valmiki who then explained to Luv and Kush that had their mother's real identity revealed; she would not have had any peace based on the stigma attached to her name by the people of Ayodhya.

Valmiki advised the boys to go to Ayodhya and question the people, as to why they tainted the good character of their mother. In that way, the people can atone for their sins. Luv and Kush took to the streets of Ayodhya and beautifully sang Rama's Katha, to the great delight and enjoyment of the people of Ayodhya. Moreover, after singing about the injustices done to their mother Sita, the people were forced to reflect and repent for their sins (Sargar).

Everywhere people gathered and talked about how foolish they had been to question the pure character of their noble Queen, Sita. They all felt a great sense of remorse for their evil thoughts about Sita. Soon the news reached the King that two young, strange boys were captivating the mind, hearts and souls of the people through their enchanted voice and song, as they sang of the glories of Rama and Sita. Thus, Rama instructed his messenger to invite the boys to his Chamber.

Rama was surprised to see that it was the same two boys, Luv and Kush whose valor and strength defeated the army of Ayodhya and was now captivating the people of Ayodhya with their sweet voices and song. Luv and Kush also informed Rama that their Guru Valmiki had written his life story and that is the story they sang. Rama was pleased and highly commended Valmiki's work who had written most beautifully.

As the boys gazed on the loving countenance of their father, their innocent hearts longed for his love and affection. Rama also felt great affection towards Luv and Kush and lovingly clasped them to his bosom. Then, Rama suggested that they spend a few days at the Palace. He advised they can recite the beautiful *Katha* every evening as composed by their Guru Valmiki for the listening enjoyment of all. Luv and Kush delightfully agreed to the King's request.

The King and the Royal family including their preceptors, King Janak, and other invited Kings, as well as the people of Ayodhya gathered at the Hall. Hearing of the "magic spell" that the young boys casted on the people, all eyes were fixed on the doorway as they anxiously awaited the arrival of Luv and Kush. As Luv and Kush entered, they were presented with Royal scarves as a gift from the King. Rama's mother Kaushalya, having laid eyes on the boys, was bewildered as she claimed that she felt as if Rama had taken a child form again (Sargar).

Having seated themselves comfortably, Luv and Kush paid their respect to the Royal family, Gurus, other respected elders and prayed that their Guru, Valmiki's blessings be upon all. Likewise, the family Guru, Vashistha returned similar blessings to Luv and Kush, as well as their Guru and Mother.

Invoking the blessing of Lord Ganesh, Goddess Saraswati, Guru Valmiki and their parents, Luv and Kush commenced the beautiful rendition of *Ramayan* that recounted the significant events of Lord Rama in sequential order. Their sweet voices, flowing rhythm and the beautiful lyrics captivated the hearts of all. Then came the sad reality as the boys sang of the great injustice done to their noble, innocent Queen, Sita who was wrongfully accused and casted out of the Kingdom. Many became very emotional as tears streamed down their cheeks, even the Gurus whose mind was of an ascetic nature, were also deeply touched.

Further, Luv and Kush alighted from their seats and slowly walked towards their father, King Rama as they sang of Sita's sufferings and the conditions under which she lived. Contrary to her Royal status, she was totally deprived of all Royal comforts. Through rain or shine, she cut and gathered fire sticks from the forest with her two young boys, fetched water from the lake, slept on the hard ground, cooked in an earthen firepit amidst the smoke that emanated from the firesticks that hurted her eyes.

King Janak was overwhelmed with grief on hearing of the harsh conditions endured by his tender Princess, Sita. Likewise, were the Mothers and the Royal family, especially Lakshman who adored his *bhabi* as his own mother. He felt her pain as she left the Palace, but was helpless to defend her plight in adherence to Royal decorum.

As their rendition came close to the end, Luv and Kush introduced themselves as the sons of Sita and Rama to the delight of the Royal family, King Janak, Guru Vashistha and Viswamitra. Rama, with deep emotions fixed his gaze affectionately towards his sons, but then quickly recollected himself as though he believed the boys, he knew the people (*Ayodhya vaasi*) would ask for proof.

Rightfully so, as the rendition ended, to the surprise of Luv and Kush, the Royal family and other distinguished Guests, some people started to express their views. Some believed the children while others asked for Sita to present herself to prove it. After listening to the mixed reactions of the people, King Rama advised the boys to bring their mother along to prove that they were his sons, as only then he can accept them and Sita.

Privately, Kaushalya scolded Rama for not embracing his sons. However, Rama reminded his mother that he had to abandon his personal feelings as He was bounded by Royal protocol. He added, that she saw the reactions of the people present and there may be more who would react negatively to the truth of the matter.

Thus, He was once again forced to endorse the *will* of the people by asking for proof, despite his own belief that undoubtedly, Luv and Kush were his sons. The great Sage Valmiki saw it all through his "divine vision" and communicated to his disciples of the mockery the people of Ayodhya are making of a virtuous woman's character.

Luv and Kush arrived home and related it all to their Guru Valmiki. Then, Valmiki requested Sita to support her husband by agreeing to testify to her purity in the courtroom of Ayodhya. He added, that Rama knows that she was pure, but he only asked for proof as that was the condition given by the people to remove their doubts.

Sita affirmed in her mind that this was the limit as she was not going to subject herself to any more pain and suffering, in light of all the test she had been through. Thus, firmly she assured the Sage that she would support her husband after which she will leave no room for doubts.

Sita's return to Mother Earth

Sita and her sons, Luv and Kush accompanied by the Great Sage Valmiki entered the Court of Ayodhya as the Royal Family, sages, and people sat in anticipation awaiting Sita's testimony. Valmiki led the way and decided to testify first on Sita's behalf to protect her from further ridicule and embarrassment. Through his "divine insight" he already knew the outcome of Sita's testimony. Thus, to avoid the matter and situation from getting worst, Valmiki testified that the boys are indeed Rama's sons as he only accepted Sita in his ashram knowing that she was pure (Sargar).

Unfortunately, Valmiki's testimony was not sufficient, and Rama still requested that Sita provide evidence as per the request of the people. A sad, pitiable, Sita fixed her eyes on the ground as she stood before the Court. However, on hearing Rama's words, she immediately looked at him with utmost firmness as if her eyes were communicating to him *'this is the limit and this is where it ends'*!

Sita slowly proceeded forth to the dismay of her close relatives and father, Janak. The younger ones bowed in reverence to her, while the Queen Mothers and King Janak indicated their love to reach out and embrace Her to their bosom. As Sita reached the middle of the Courtroom, she grievingly paid her respects to the exalted Gurus and Preceptors, Queen Mothers, King Janak and King Rama.

According to Tulsidas, Sita then testified that *"she had not known any other man, but Rama nor has she ever thought of another man as she only worshipped her Lord Rama in thought, word and deed, mind body and soul. She further declared that if her words are true, then may Mother Earth accept her in her lap instantly"* (Sargar).

Sita's firm words struck like lightning, and everyone looked at her in awe and bewilderment as none expected of her such a powerful, proclamation. Instantly, like an earthquake, the ground beside her opened, and up emerged Mother Earth seated in her Throne. Sita with clasped hands and tears streaming down her tender cheeks beseeched Mother Earth to deliver her from her distress. Moreover, Sita claimed that she had been through many tests and she was now so tired. Mother Earth felt her deep distress and with outstretched arms invited Sita to come to her loving embrace. Sita Devi willing obliged and Mother Earth lovingly embraced her.

Sita turned to her respected elders and bid them farewell. She then imparted her last lessons to her beloved sons. She entrusted Luv and Kush to their father and advised them that serving him lies their greatest blessings. Finally, she paid her respect to her beloved husband, Rama and prayed that in all her future births to have him as her husband, but begged of him to not let anything like that happen again (Sargar).

Rama tried to stop Sita from leaving, but she begged him to not stop her as it was her time to return home. Mother Earth then seated Sita beside her and assured Sita that no one will ever be able to hurt her again. In that way, Mother Earth's Throne descended, and the opened ground fastened, thus leaving everyone in shock and tears. When a quiet, righteous and innocent person is falsely accused and criticized repeatedly, God will certainly deliver and grant justice to such a noble soul.

Rama rushed forth in an attempt to stop Sita from leaving, but to no avail. Then, he begged Mother Earth to return his Sita; after which he threatened to destroy the Earth. Instantly, Lord Brahma appeared and advised Rama to introspect on his Divinity and his purpose as he incarnated to save the Earth from the oppression of Ravan, not destroy the Earth. Hence, Rama recollected himself, and Valmiki offered him wise counsel. Valmiki added that through his 'divine vision" he knew that would happen, but though he tried he was unable to prevent it.

The wise Sage further advised Rama to take care of Sita's treasures Luv and Kush that she entrusted to him. With that sound advice, Valmiki communicated to Luv and Kush that his duty by them is over. Subsequently, he bestowed his blessings on Luv and Kush, and everyone as he bid them farewell. Rama lovingly clasped his sons, Luv and Kush to his bosom. Moreover, Luv and Kush were warmly received by the Royal Family and were given their rightful place in the Kingdom. Beautifully decked with Royal attire and jewelry, they shone forth as charming young Princes of Ayodhya.

Rama returns to Vaikuntha

As time passed, one day Kaal (the incarnation of time) paid a secret visit to Rama. He informed King Rama that what he was about to communicate to him is "top secret". Therefore they both need to be alone. Kaal also requested Rama to take an oath that if anyone were to enter the room, that person would be sentenced to death. Rama agreed and asked Lakshman to stand guard at the door and to not allow anyone in under any condition.

Kaal informed Lord Rama that he was sent by Maha Vishnu Bhagwan, the Sustainer of the Universe to remind him that the allotted time span for his stay on Earth was almost over. Thus, he should prepare for his ascend to his divine abode, *Vaikuntha*. As Lakshman stood guard, Durvasa Muni arrived and asked to meet with Sri Rama. Lakshman politely explained that Rama was in an important meeting and asked not to be disturbed.

Moreover, Lakshman humbly requested Durvasa to wait for awhile and then he can meet with Rama, but the short-tempered Durvasa insisted that he meets with Rama immediately. Recalling Rama's strict instructions and moreso, the consequences of breaking the rules, Lakshman tried politely again and again to deter Durvasa which further aroused his anger.

An angry Durvasa threatened that if Lakshman does not allow him to promptly meet with Rama, he will burn the City of Ayodhya with his Divine powers. Lakshman became terrified of Durvasa's wrath and moreso, faced with such a dilemma. If he allowed Durvasa to enter, not only will Lakshman disobey King Rama's instructions, but he will receive the death sentence. On the other hand, if he does not allow Durvasa to instantly meet with Rama, Durvasa will burn the City with his fury.

Thinking thus, Lakshman decided on the wise choice of the matter to sacrifice his life for the protection and welfare of Ayodhya and its people. Thus, Lakshman entered the room to the dismay of Rama and Kaal, who instantly disappeared. He informed the King of Durvasa's arrival and reluctance to wait to meet with him.

Although King Rama was a bit annoyed with Lakshman for having disobeyed his instructions, Rama understood the sound reasoning. However, Rama was bounded by his word and oath to Kaal and had to discharge his duty by punishing Lakshman. Hence, King Rama sat in consultation with his Guru Vashistha, brothers and the wise Hanuman. They brainstorm for other equivalent punishment to the dealth penalty, as Lakshman was a blood relative and a first time offender. As such, Rama wanted to be somewhat lenient to his faithful, Lakshman while at the same time to honor his given word to Kaal.

In this regard, the wise, merciful Hanuman who was versed in the Vedas proposed that scriptures declare that *renouncing a relative is equivalent to the death sentence.* Hence, Hanuman suggested renouncing Lakshman which was unanimously agreed upon, and thus, King Rama sadly renounced Lakshman. A grieving Lakshman feasted his eyes on his beloved brother Rama for the last time, as it was the very first time in his (Lakshman's) life that he was being separated from his dearly, beloved brother, Rama. Then Lakshman proceeded to the Sarayu River and taking a dip; he adopted his original form of *Sheesnag* and returned to *Vaikuntha.*

In due time, all 8 Princes, (Rama and his 3 brothers were all blessed with twin boys) became noble, responsible young men. Hence, King Rama equally divided the different States of Ayodhya among the eight young Princes to govern the various cities. Thus, handing over the responsibilities of the Kingdom in that way, Rama prepared for his exit from the mortal world.

Rama proceeded to meet with his Guru Vashistha at his ashram to seek his blessings, as he prepared for his divine abode in *Vaikuntha*

Lok. A large group of people from the city followed him there and begged their King Rama to accompany him as well. They claimed Ayodhya would be bereft without him, and thus does not hold any meaning for them.

With hearts full of love for the Lord they sadly supplicated before Rama with folded palms. Guru Vashistha advised Rama to accept them as was his compassionate nature to fulfill the heart desires of his devotees. Rama with a sweet, beautiful smile on his lips lovingly obliged. They all followed behind Rama as he proceeded to the Sarayu River to the chants of praises to Maha Vishnu Bhagwan.

Taking a dip in the Sarayu River, Rama adopted his original 4-arm form of Maha Vishnu Bhagwan to the delight of all as they beheld the most beauteous form of Sri Hari. As the Lord mounted his seat on his vehicle, the golden eagle, Garuda, He advised Vibhishan to propitiate his form as *Nikumbula,* the deity of the demons.

Sugriv prompted that he already handed over the Kingdom to Angad as he was not staying behind without Rama. The Lord smiled lovingly and endorsed Sugriv's decision. Finally, turning to the beloved Hanuman, the Lord blessed him to stay on Earth and take care of the people as in tough days the people will need his help and support. Hanuman lovingly bowed to the Lord in reverence.

Lastly, the Lord, Sri Hari requested Lord Brahma to allow a part of his domain for his (Maha Vishnu's) many followers who were all Divine beings that had taken human form to support him on Earth. Lord Brahma gladly and readily obliged to the request of Maha Vishnu Bhagwan. In that way, Sri Rama adopted his original form of Maha Vishnu and ascended on the Golden Eagle to his divine abode.

Likewise, his followers entered into the river as well, and taking a dip they were all transformed into their Divine forms and thus, ascended to their heavenly abode. Sugriv, the King of the apes;

Sumant, the Chief Minister of Dasrath, and Guha, the King of the forest dwellers, were all Devatas in disguise. Having taken a dip in the "holy" waters of the Saruyu, they adopted their original forms and ascended to their heavenly abode. Thus, this concludes the golden epic "*Ramayan*" as documented and narrated in Tulsidas's, Sri Ramcharitamanas, and visually replicated in Sargar's Ramayan, (1987) for a clearer and better understanding of the sacred text.

Works Cited

Ramanand Sargar. *Ramayan.* (1987).

Tulsidass. Sri Ramcharitamanas. (no date).

Discussion

As shown in this narration of *Ramayan Katha*, many invaluable, divine lessons can be learnt in relation to our daily lives. The *Katha* evolved around two most powerful men, one of righteous conduct (Rama), and the other of unrighteous conduct (Ravan). Rama sacrificed his happiness by renouncing his innocent, devoted wife to please the people of Ayodhya. In contrast, Ravan sacrificed his powerful sons, brother, and people in an attempt to satisfy his ego and lust to possess another man's wife. Thus, on one hand we have a noble, selfless King (Rama) who delivered happiness to his people at all cost, whereas on the other hand, an arrogant, selfish King who caused the mass destruction of his own relatives and people.

Moreover, we have seen the highest degree of (a) a father's love for his son (Dasrath & Rama), (b) father-daughter bond (Janak & Sita), (c) brotherly love and unity (Bharat & Rama, Lakshman & Rama), (d) an ideal son (Rama), (e)an ideal daughter and mother (Sita), (f) most devoted and dutiful wives (Sita, Kaushalya & Mandodari), (g) the highest degree of humility and nobility of two powerful families in wedlock (Dasrath & Janak), (h) mother-in-law and daughter-in-law loving relationship (Kaushalya & Sita), (i) unconditional love and utmost loyalty of a loving wife and husband (Sita & Rama), (j) the performance of one's duty (Rama), (k) humility and steadfast devotion to the Divine Lord (Hanuman, Bharat & Lakshman), (l) truth, righteousness, selflessness (Rama, Sita, Bharat, Lakshman & Hanuman), (m) true friendship (Sugriv & Rama), and (n) the cost of ego and lust of a man to possess a woman (Ravan).

As parents, although work, wealth, name, fame and the pleasures of the world might be of great significance, our children are our real treasures. Although King Dasrath was well known for control over his 10 senses, hence his given name, when it comes to his most beloved son, Rama, he was overpowered by emotions which ultimately led to his unfortunate demise. Similarly, King Janak was known for his calm disposition as nothing could evoke his emotions, but parting from his most beloved daughter, Sita on her wedding day, significantly triggered his emotions.

Such is the infinite power of pure love that captivated the hearts of powerful Emperors like Dasrath and Janak, and Great Ascetics like Vashistha and Valmiki. Moreover, through pure love and devotion as exemplified by Bharat, Lakshman, and Hanuman to Rama, the Lord that controls this entire cosmos is conquered and thus, dwells within the confines of the heart of a *true devotee*. Thus, as Rama stated, our love for God and our dear ones should be unconditional. We should do good things and not talk about it nor expect anything in return. According to Mother Theresa *"intense love does not measure, it just gives"*.

When brothers can maintain that close bond and live in peace and harmony with one another, such a relationship will never collapse even with the greatest difficulty that may come their way. Such was the unconditional brotherly love and unity demonstrated by the four brothers, Rama, Bharat, Lakshman and Shatrughna that is beyond compare, as the four brothers walked the path of truth and righteous conduct. Hence, their strong bond was unbreakable, despite the many challenges they faced.

For example, Kaikeyi advocated for Bharat to crown King, instead of Rama, which separated the loving brothers. However, neither Bharat nor Rama developed any animosity or hatred towards one other as their deep love for each other was beyond name, fame and wealth. Moreover, out of unconditional love, Lakshman chose to stand by his righteous brother in his time of distress, thus giving up all material wealth, comfort and marital pleasures to accompany his brother to the forest.

Parents work hard and make many sacrifices to provide the best of everything for their children, but yet, expects nothing in return, only that their children always stay safe, healthy and happy. As Lataji beautifully sang, "Oh Maa, Oh Maa...tu kitni achhi hai". She stated, *"A mother's joy or sorrow is not hers, as when her child cries, she cries and when her child laughs, she laughs. Thus, for the laughter and tears of her child, a mother sacrifices for it all"*.

Sri Rama was the ideal son, who not only made his parents proud, but the people of Ayodhya as he made all the right choices by them. For example, when Kaikeyi requested the two boons, Dasrath was too grief-stricken to uphold his given word to Kaikeyi, but Rama recognized his duty by his father in that highly, sensitive situation. However, Kaikeyi loved Rama as much as her son Bharat, but she was a victim of *Maya* (illusion), as Destiny decreed and seized total control of her good sense and rationality. According to Tulsidasji, Ramayan declares that *"no one is clever or foolish, but acts in accordance to the will of fate at a given time"*.

Thus, when a decent person unbelievably commits a mistake, he /she must not be treated with contempt, as we must not forget the 99 good things over the one unfortunate mistake that such a person may unknowingly commit. Personally, I like to weigh the good and the bad and to alway focus on the brighter side of things, as with many unfortunate situations, there must be a bright, underlining side, sometimes known or unknown to us.

Rama took on the responsibility of honoring his father's given word and decided to leave for the forest, thus adding glory to his father's name, as well as, the *Raghukul Dynasty*. Moreover, a dispassionate Rama with a guileless heart stood firm on his resolve and adhere to all the rules of his exile while casting out blame on anyone. Many a time, one is quick to blame others for one's downfall or mistakes, rather than examine one's thoughts and actions to find answers.

Like Rama, Sita was the ideal daughter of Janak, who was obedient and honored her parent's words and reputation. For example, she observed decorum and upheld her father's vow, even when at first sight she helplessly *fell in love* with Rama. She placed her desire at the feet of the Goddess Bhavani, but never asked for Rama's hand in marriage. When children respect and honor the good upbringing by their parents, such children will accomplish great things in life.

Such was the extreme level of discipline of Janaki (Sita) as she was lovingly referred to because of the close father-daughter bond. Her charming personality and righteous conduct captivated the hearts of all, but unfortunately, she was the object of many tests, trials and sacrifices. Although Sita was repeatedly faced with despair and injustices, she held firm to her beliefs, morals and integrity. Hence, she made her parents, countrymen and in-laws proud and thus, left behind a *Distinction* in the world of an ideal daughter, wife, and mother for womankind.

Sita was an ideal wife who was devoted to her husband in thought, word and deed, despite being separated from Rama. For example, although Ravan tried repeatedly to entice her in many ways, she angrily shunned his offers as material wealth and luxury meant nothing for her as compared to her love for her Lord Rama. Afterall, she was a Princess who was married to a Prince, but she gave up all luxury and comfort to stand at the side of her beloved husband.

Though being a single parent to her babies, Sita was a loving, ideal mother who instilled in her children moral and spiritual values to become self-made, independent young men. She reinforced the lessons taught by their Guru/teacher. She also taught her children about obedience and ethical conduct towards their Guru/teacher, parents, respected elders, fellow human beings and the world. Sita engaged her boys in daily domestic and household chores, as such basic skills are meant for both boys and girls to learn for their own benefit.

Luv and Kush, though mere boys conquered the mighty army of Ayodhya including mighty warriors like Lakshman and Bharat who were incomparable in strength and prowess. This symbolizes, when children have an excellent teacher, both at home and at school, they would reach the highest pinnacle of education and success in this world. That means, the lesson taught at school must be reinforced at home as parents and teachers must cooperate and collaborate to maximize learning for students' and to also incorporate discipline along the way so that they become *assets* to Society.

Further, in this education era, research has shown that parental engagement in their children's learning, growth and development stimulates, and enriches learning for children to succeed. Moreso, parental support motivates children to better engage in learning, and encourage and inspire them to attend school regularly, and to learn. Moreover, while technological support promotes student's learning and enhances academic performances, it is important to note that supervision is necessary to achieve the intended outcome.

Every parent desire an ideal son or daughter who would add glory to their name and make them proud. Therefore, it is incumbent upon parents to discipline and teach their children to be good human beings, as no child is born a criminal or sinner. However, discipline does not mean corporal punishment or severe physical abuse on children. Children are innocent, delicate human beings, who deserve love and respect and should be treated thus, as the future generation. It must be noted that children learn good or bad behavior from the adults around them.

Thus, discipline should be done in a civilized way, so that children can learn through our example of how to love, respect and treat others. Therefore, we must always try to instill in our children good morals, spiritual values, and ethical conduct from a young age. Just as how we mould and shape a young plant in the desired direction, so too we need to train our children, and guide them in the right direction, as the older they grow, the more difficult it becomes to change their course. Thus, when we teach our children to follow the right path of life, they would grow to make wise choices in life and thus, reap the rewards.

The marriage ceremony of Sita and Rama was not just the union of two souls, but the union of two noble families of equal status. Both Dasrath and Janak took turns in praising one another for the good fortune of begetting a virtuous spouse for their son/daughter. Such was the humility and grace of the two storehouses of nobility in the form of Dasrath and Janak that history failed to distinguish which one was the real beneficiary of good fortune.

While weddings are usually a most joyous occasion, it can be quite painful for the parents of the bride in particular, as a daughter leaves her nuptial home with her husband. However, when parents are satisfied that their daughter has begotten a suitable match and settles in a good home, whereby in-laws treat their children as their own, that comforts the aching heart and eliminates the worry of parents.

Such was the loving relationship that Kaushalya shared with Sita to the extent that Kaushalya lovingly supported Sita's arguments to accompany her husband to the forest, over her son Rama's refusal to take Sita along as well. Kaushalya also shared the deep grief of her beloved daughter-in-law, Sita who was cast out of the Kingdom. Sita too respected and adored her husband's parents as her parents.

As Rama emphasized, when a man dons a crown, he is bounded by the *will and mandate* of the people. That means if the need arises, he must be willing to sacrifice his happiness for the happiness of others. The Monarchs of the Raghukul Dynasty demonstrated this unique type of selfless rulership. For example, despite the faithful, pure, deep love that Sita and Rama cherished for each other, Rama was forced to renounce his innocent, beloved wife to please the people of Ayodhya.

There are those who are quick to criticize others conveniently, but fail to examine and reflect on their faults and shortcomings. Some people misunderstood Rama's helpless position, as they criticized Rama for what they perceived as "believing the people and accusing his innocent wife of infidelity". However, one must be mindful that although Rama acted as an ordinary mortal, He was not separated from his Divine Reality. That means, Rama performed many divine tasks that is uncommon for an ordinary man.

Here are some examples, (a) He immediately recognized Sati when she disguised as Sita, (b) The mere touch of his feet transformed a stone into a woman, (c) He gave Hanuman his ring to present to Sita in Lanka, (d) He slept on a grass mat on the floor to share in the pain and sufferings of his beloved wife in the forest, (e) He sent Shatrughna to perform the necessary *sanskaar*/ritual on his behalf at the birth of his sons, (f) He refused to remarry as he believed his wife was pure and innocent, and so more.

How did Rama know that Hanuman would be the one to find Sita? How did he know that a grass mat was prepared for his wife to sleep on the ground and thus, simultaneously instructed Lakshman to make one for him as well? How did he know about the exact timing of the birth of his babies to send Shatrughna to represent him? Was it all coincidence? Are these the acts of an ordinary mortal as Rama portrayed? How then can one conclude that he doubted his wife's purity? Would Rama conveniently believe the people's accusation of such a cruel stigma on his wife's pure character, as well as his noble character for believing the people over his wife?

Moreover, Rama was the very epitome of truth, duty, righteousness and selflessness. How then can he be categorized as the dim-witted Dooby who accused his innocent wife of infidelity? Is there any link or comparison between a man of wisdom and character (Rama) and a man of ignorance and arrogance (Dooby)? Is it then valid or justifiable to conclude that a man of such caliber as Rama doubted his wife's purity? Further, it must be taken into consideration that when the Guru and Brahmanas advised Rama to remarry as critical to perform the *Ashwamedh Yagna*, Rama immediately rebuked the idea and argued that his beloved wife, Sita is innocent. Does this not clarify that Rama ***never*** believed the people's false accusations about his wife?

When a man joins the army, fire service or police force, he pledges to sacrifice his life if necessary to serve and protect the people. That means that his duty by his Countrymen is of "top priority" over his personal and family life. For example, if a close relative of a Police Officer is being accused of a crime, the Policeman is expected to rise above his emotions as is his *prime duty* to arrest his own relative, regardless of his personal feelings. If this is understandable, then why is it so difficult for some people to understand Rama's position regarding his foremost, prime duty, firstly as a King over his duty as a husband?

Furthermore, many Fire Officers readily sacrificed their lives at the urgent call to discharge their *prime duty* to save people from the 9/11 terrorist attack on the United States in 2001. Similarly, as a King or a Leader, Rama was duty-bound by the people's *will and mandate* as is a requirement of a just and righteous Leader, moreso an Emperor of his particular esteemed lineage. Hence, the reason he was forced to sacrifice his happiness by renouncing his beloved wife, in spite of knowing that she was pure and innocent.

In contrast, Rama clearly emphasized that this Royal protocol does not apply to a common man. Rather, a common man's *prime duty* is to take care of his wife, children, and extended family. Moreso, a common man should not be negatively influenced by other people on how to run the affairs of his household.

We live in a challenging Society whereby, whether we do something or not, people may say good things or sometimes may falsely accuse us. Moreover, there may be few individuals who think that they know about the reasons for our choices and actions more than us, and thus draw their own absurd conclusions. We all know what is best for our respective families and household, and as such, we must not be intimidated or bothered by the false accusations or bias opinions of others.

Further, despite the challenges we may face along life's journey, we must not falter or lose our focus on our vision and mission in life. As hard as we try to lead an honest and decent life, there will always be few like Manthara who would still find faults in us. Thus, we must not be deterred by the minority, but be encouraged by the majority who truly loves and appreciates us, and stay firm on our path. On the other hand, constructive criticism forces and helps us to reflect and introspect, to create and foster positive social changes in our lives which will ultimately make us stronger and wiser human beings.

I grew up hearing people criticize Sita for crossing the line drawn by Lakshman. They fail to understand that a devoted and faithful wife, as Sita would do everything in her power to safeguard her husband from harm, injury or death. Ravan, whom she believed to be a Holy man threatened to pronounce a curse on Rama through which the sharp horns of the deer will pierce his body and kill him, had Sita not presented the alms to the cunning Ravan where he was seated. Hence, she crossed the line to protect her beloved husband from injury and death, as she believed at that moment in time.

Further, many people also criticize Rama for putting Sita through the *"fire test"* before taking her rightful place at his side after Sri Rama's victory in the war against Ravan. However, one must be very mindful that pure and chaste women like Sita, Anusuriya, and Vrinda upheld such high ideals of *"pativraata dharma"* or devoted wifehood, that the mere touch of another man would have made them impure. Hence, the reason as Sita explained to Hanuman that despite her deep distress under Ravan's custody, she could not leave with him. Moreover, Sita represented the Universal Mother on Earth acting as an ordinary mortal.

Sita Maata represents *Maha Shakti* which is the absolute power of all creations in the Universe. If a mere line drawn by Lakshman emanated electric sparks that Ravan was unable to cross, could he then, even touch the real Sita who was absolute power personified? I think he would have been instantly burnt to ashes. Hence, the real Sita was kept in the safe custody of the Fire God, Agni Devata, while an illusionary Sita was created to portray her role. Thus, after the Lord's purpose in the forest was fully accomplished, including the destruction of Ravan, Rama retrieved his beloved wife from the Fire God, Agni Devata.

The friendship between Rama and Sugriv was such an ideal example of what trust and true friendship entails. They helped each other tremendously in their times of distress and celebrated their respective victory together. Rama stressed that a friend's enemy was also his enemy, and thus He slew Bali. However, I think it is worth pondering that had Bali also been a friend of Rama, would the outcome be the same? Would Rama have incurred enmity with Bali to please and favor Sugriv? Would he have killed Bali? I think

Rama would have taken the necessary steps to reunite the two brothers, while Sugriv receives justice and Bali repents for his sins.

The utmost love and steadfast devotion to Rama as characterized by the humble Hanuman; noble Bharat; and faithful Lakshman are most highly commendable and incomparable to others. Although Bharat and Lakshman, amidst immense challenges and sacrifices lovingly and selflessly served their elder brother and King, Rama, it was the humble and devoted Hanuman who was the messenger of Rama and thus, accomplished all the impossible tasks.

Hanuman was always present to help those in distress. Without telling him what needed to be done, he used his own discretion and intelligence and thus, acted accordingly without delay, bringing relief to those in need. Such is the generous nature of our beloved, Hanuman who is most present in this age, *Kaliyug* to help us, as *"Rama's words hold the highest truth"*. Thus, whenever our hearts are overburden with distress and our efforts seems limited to bring relief, turn to God in prayer and place your troubles at his feet, as some problems are better left in the hands of God.

Aside from Hanuman's divine reality of being the 11th incarnation of Lord Shiva, with Rama enshrined in his heart, he always placed the Lord first and chanted his name before embarking on any task. As such, nothing was impossible for the wise and mighty Hanuman to accomplish. Thus, he was always successful in every undertaking despite the challenges that came his way. Many great things in life comes with added challenges and sacrifices. Wherever we set out to accomplish something good, we often face hurdles and may need to make sacrifices. Greater the achievement, the harder the task to be performed, and greater the sacrifices. Let's take for example, a primary level test as compared to a tertiary level exam.

When we thread on the path of truth and righteousness, though a difficult narrow path to keep steady, we will certainly achieve our purpose, despite being faced with challenges and hurdles along the way as exemplified by Hanuman. Therefore, like Sita, parents must take the time to teach their children well, to withstand any storm that may come their way, so that they may not quiver or be blown away by a strong wind.

In other words, children must be taught to persevere, be resilient, and determined, so that they can achieve their goals independently of others. In that way, they can fend for themselves and stand strong on their own, amidst all the challenges and difficulties that may come their way along life's journey. Guru Vashistha taught Sri Rama and his brothers this important lesson. Hence, they survived well despite the harsh conditions of living in the forest.

Like Sita, both Kaushalya and Mandodari were among the most virtuous wives who totally worshipped and adored their husbands, Dasrath, and Ravan respectively. It is very important to note that, although Ravan was an unrighteous King, Mandodari maintained her virtue and faithfulness towards her husband. Therefore, if a man chooses to walk on the sinful path, it does not mean that his wife or family have to support his wrongdoings or follow suit with him. For example, Visbhishan was also of the demon race, but he chose to lead a noble and righteous life in devotion to God.

Similarly, Prahalad was the son of the demon Hiranyakashipu, but he was also a pure devotee of Lord Vishnu. Hiranyakashipu tried in many ways to kill Prahalad, but young Prahalad was protected by the Lord. Finally, the combined strengths of Lord Vishnu, and Lord Shiva manifested as *Narasimha Bhagwan* and killed the wicked demon, Hiranyakashipu. Therefore, we all possess the ability to rise above immoral behavior and unethical conduct of one's family and the home, to transform our lives, *like the lotus flower that grows in the mud, yet it rises above the mud, and is neither stained nor blemished.* More importantly, the lotus flower is most beautiful to delight the eyes, and it is offered at the sacred feet of God in prayer. Therefore, we must refrain from casting aspersions or judgment on others based on their physical appearance or family background.

Mandodari completely understood Sita's plight and was thus, kind and felt pity for her as she recognized in Sita, another faithful and devoted wife as herself. However, Ravan disregarded Mandodari's good counsel at every step of the way and thus, through his ego and lust to forcibly possess another's wife, He was slained. Mandodari's purity protected Ravan to a great extent until he overstepped his bounds by creating enmity with the Lord of the Universe, Sri Rama.

Similarly, in a related *katha*, the demon King Jalandhar who was unmatched in strength was protected by his wife, Vrinda's purity. He immensely created havoc on Earth, and thus as the *devatas* concluded, the only way to slay him was to break his wife's purity. Hence, the Lord had to intervene to destroy one heinous criminal to protect the people. One must not allow the intoxicating power of false pride and ego to cloud one's critical thinking and judgment, but to clearly rationalize and distinguish between right and wrong and thus, be guided in that way.

Tears flowed from the *lotus-eye* of the Sustainer of the Universe, Maha Vishnu Bhagwan. He was forced to take such an unjust step against his devotee, Vrinda for the protection and happiness of the people of the world. Therefore, the Lord took the form of Vrinda's husband and embraced her. Jalandhar was immediately slained by Lord Shiva in the battlefield. Vrinda thus, having recognized the deceit of the Lord, Maha Vishnu, pronounced a curse on him to become a stone as she accused him of being stone-hearted to have deceived her.

Consequently, the Lord adopted the form of the *Shaligram* (a small oval-shaped, black stone, worshipped in Sri Satnarayan pooja). Further, the compassionate Lord blessed Vrinda to be reborn as the sacred *Tulsi Plant* and moreover, pledged that He would not accept any offerings made to him without a *Tulsi leaf*. Thus, the merciful Lord Vishnu elevated Vrinda to such extent of having everlasting life and eternal companionship with him.

While we are expected not to disown or betray a close relative, even if they adopt evil ways, they must be willing to change and atone for their sins. However, Ravan resisted change and, thus Vibhishan chose to thread on the path of truth and righteousness for the well-being and protection of his people. Hence, Vibhishan did not betray his brother Ravan, but the bitter consequences of Ravan's evil actions resulted in a battle of *good versus evil*. Similarly, in the *Mahabarat* war, Arjuna was encouraged and supported by Bhagwan Krishna to bravely fight against his own relatives, as it was also, a battle of *righteousness over unrighteousness*. In both cases, Vibhishan and Arjuna chose to uphold dharma as *"truth must always prevail"*.

Conclusion

As we have gathered Rama and Sita as well as other members of the Royal Family led a most truthful and righteous life, yet they were faced with tremendous sufferings and pain. However, that was a result of mainly the *Raghukul Culture* and *Royal Protocol,* as well as their *Past Karma (deeds) and Fate (destiny).* Similarly, we also experience difficulties and challenges along life's journey, based on past, and present karma and fate, but how we deal with it makes the difference. That is, what we should *do* and *not do* in our times of distress are explicitly documented in our sacred *Ramayan* as briefly explained herein, thus no need to reiterate.

In this time and context, when we choose to live a life of truth and righteousness that includes **God**, we will experience more joy than sorrow and more success than failure in our life. I can testify to this as God always provide for the needs of his devotees, *"as what the devotee wants, the devotee gets"*. However, we must always cherish legitimate desires that are attainable, knowing that the source of happiness may vary from one person to the other. That is, what makes one person happy may not necessarily make another person happy.

Through intense devotion, God can change the course of destiny in the life of a pure, ardent devotee. For example, in the *Markandeya Katha*, through steadfast worship of the devotee, Markandeya, he was blessed by Lord Shiva with very long life, preceding the boon granted to Markandeya's parents that their son would live only for 16 years. Such is the compassionate nature of the Lord to even bend the rules out of love for his ardent devotees.

In this rapidly changing diverse world of technology and science, education is crucial for survival, and happiness. Simultaneously, it is critically important that we teach our children to include God in their daily lives, taking into consideration the cruel things that can sometimes happen in an instant to innocent children. Therefore, that ultimate protection of our dearly, beloved children can only come from God who is omniscient, omnipresent and omnipotent.

Filmmakers today are doing great work, combining the lessons of our religious texts through *cartoon and animation* to fully engage the interest of young children, and thus facilitate their learning of our *dharma/religion.* However, parents must get involved and scrutinize the contents as some parts could be misleading and pose serious harm to young children who likes to model *"Super Hero"* characters. In an animated series of the *Holy Ramayan,* I saw where Rama removed one of his eyes to make up the 1000 lotuses to appease Goddess Durga. What impact would this scene have on the innocent minds of young children?

I am not aware of any such scenes in the *Ramayan,* but in another *Katha,* Lord Vishnu was short of one lotus flower to make up a 1000 lotuses to perform a special *pooja/ritual* to Lord Shiva. He then recalled that his devotees refer to him as *"Kamalanayan"* the lotus-eyed one. Hence, as Lord Vishnu attempted to remove one of his eyes, Lord Shiva appeared and indicated to Lord Vishnu that there was no need for such a cruel sacrifice to propitiate him. Lord Shiva was pleased with the love and devotion of Lord Vishnu and blessed him to achieve his purpose.

Dearly beloved children, God does not want you to do anything that is harmful to you, but only your love and devotion. The merciful Lord is most pleased with simple offerings, such as *water, flower, leave, fruit and love,* as declared by Bhagwan Krishna in *Bhagwat Gita.* For example, the arrogant Prince Duryodhan invited Lord Krishna for a lavish meal prepared with pride. Simultaneously, the humble and righteous Vidur prepared a simple meal with love and invited Krishna as well. Thus, Lord Krishna went to Vidur's sacred home and partook of the vegetables and rice prepared with love.

We all came into this world with *"atma-gyaan"* or *"knowledge of the soul"* which is our discriminating power to distinguish between good and bad or right and wrong. Aside from our *past karma* or actions, the choices we make in life helps determine our future destiny, and also the extent of our joy or sorrow along life's journey. Therefore, it is always individual choice as to whether we choose to make the right choices and reap the merits/rewards, or bad choices and suffer the penalties. That is, when we make good decisions in life we enjoy the benefits and rewards it brings our way towards the fulfillment of our hearts desires and goals. On the other hand, when we make poor choices/decisions, one has to endure the unfavorable consequences of it that may seldom offer temporary happiness, but will ultimately lead to unhappiness and self-destruction.

In the lives of us, ordinary human beings, we may never know what another is thinking or how one feels about things or situations. That is because every individual is unique and thus, perceive things and life in different ways based on one's culture, beliefs, knowledge, and experiences. Hence, we should kindly accept and appreciate others for who they are and what they are, as well as tolerate and respect the likes, dislikes and preferences of others in this globally diverse world.

When faced with difficulties and matters of the heart, it is essential to seek divine guidance from God and to also confide in someone that genuinely cares, for advice and direction to move forward. No problem in life is too big to solve through God's blessings and good counsel from parents, guru/teacher, trusted family members and friends. Our parents are our God on Earth as they brought us into this world and lovingly provides for our every need and protection. Therefore, our parents are like Creator, Sustainer and Protector to us on Earth. Thus, we must cherish our parents while they are in this world and never make the mistake of casting them out of our lives, as we may never know when will be their last day with us.

Further, it is only when we have children of our own, we will truly understand the countless challenges and sacrifices of parenthood. Thus, how then can we remain angry with our parents in light of how much they did for us and continue to do, out of unconditional love for us. Long ago, the challenge lied in basically providing food, clothing and shelter for our children, but now the basic challenges lies moreso, in providing our children with higher education in a most competent world, while keeping them safe from diseases and evildoers.

Lord Ganesh has beautifully demonstrated how we should honor and worship our parents. Lord Ganesh was placed in a contest with his brother Kartikeya, to go around the world. While Kartikeya took flight on his peacock, the intelligent Lord Ganesh circumambulated his parents 3 times representing the three worlds - *Heaven, Earth*, and the *Netherworld.* Thus, Lord Shiva and Goddess Parvati were tremendously pleased of the wisdom that Ganesha possesses, even as a young boy.

Through sincere devotion to God and noble efforts to achieve our goals, anything that is legitimate and right for us is possible, as our beloved Hanuman has taught us. Although God is omniscient, and everything belongs to him, we must take the time to express our love and gratitude to him. For instance, we take for granted the love of our family members, and thus we rarely expresses our feelings to one another. However, when we are presented with a token or gift of love and appreciation, it makes quite a difference, right? Moreso, the more unique the gift, the happier the recipient, isn't it?

Although God is not limited to the dualities of this mortal world, he is captivated by the expressions of love of his devotees. That means the more we express our love to him, the more pleased is the Lord. For example, contrary to our belief as Hindus that we should not taste anything that is meant to offer to God as *"prasadam"* or food,

Rama ate the berries that Shabari bitten and offered to him with love.

Similarly, in *Bhagwat Katha*, the poor Brahmin, Sudama once visited his childhood friend, Krishna. When Lord Krishna who was the King of Dwarika heard of the arrival of his childhood friend, Sudama, Krishna rushed forth to meet him. Everyone present was bewildered because Sudama appeared as a beggar. Krishna lovingly embraced him and inquired of Sudama if he had brought anything for him.

Sudama was too embarrassed to offer to the King, patched rice that his wife had sent for Krishna. Perceiving that Sudama was hiding something behind his back, Krishna snatched the small package wrapped with an old piece of cloth. The cloth easily tored, and the grains fell on the ground. Lord Krishna grabbed the rice and ate like a hungry person. Did the Lord of the Universe in the form of Sri Rama and Sri Krishna alike, really craved those berries and patched rice?

During their childhood, Krishna and Sudama were sent to fetch the firesticks. A thunderstorm broke out, and both climbed up a tree to pass the torrential rains. They became hungry and Sudama started greedily eating the grains that were given to them by Sudama's mother. Krishna heard the crunchy sound and inquired about it, but Sudama claimed his teeth were making that sound as he was cold. Thus, Sudama ate all the grains and did not care to share with Krishna. Perhaps, that sinful act of greediness and worst yet, lying to the Lord about it, resulted in his poverty which is the greatest unhappiness in the world, as stated by Sri Rama.

Although Lord Krishna knew the truth, he never held Sudama in contempt, but instead lovingly embraced his friend upon his visit. Similarly, Sri Rama never blamed anyone for his fate nor did he held Manthara in contempt for her actions, although she was the mastermind behind the plan to create division in the Royal Family. Therefore, although someone may have wronged us, we must not hate, but forgive them and even help them in their times of need. The wise understands that *karma* and *fate* plays a crucial role in the events of our lives, whether good or bad. Therefore, why hold others in contempt and create enmity with our near and dear ones.

The Lord is ecstatic when his devotees offer something to him with pure love and devotion. Lord Krishna blessed Sudama abundantly as upon his return home that day, instead of his little hut, he saw a mansion and his wife stood beautifully adorned at the doorway. Can anyone ever fathom the greatness and compassion of our Lord and Master? Dasrath and Kaushalya in their previous birth prayed for the Lord to be born in their home as their son. However, the compassionate Lord manifested as not one, but four virtuous sons that is symbolic of the four fruits of life - *dharma, wealth, sensuous pleasures and liberation.*

Therefore, spiritualize your lives and develop a close relationship with God. Offer your love, chant his name, sing his praises, observe fast and make offerings, especially during auspicious festivals and so forth. Those who engage in worship in this way with a guileless, pure heart and soul is '*dear to the Lord*' as declared by both, Sri Ram in *Ramayan,* and Sri Krishna in *Bhagwat Gita.* Maintain that spiritual balance as you strive to achieve your aspirations in life. Just do your best and leave the rest to God to answer your call, as God works in mysterious ways, and sometimes at the last moment.

Sri Rama & Sri Krishna

Further, one must be mindful that since we cannot see beyond our physical eyes and thus, we may not really know what might be good or not good for us, God understands and knows best. Therefore, be careful of what you pray for, as sometimes what we think is good for us may not be in our best interest. Sometimes, if we do not get what we pray for, we must not lose faith. Rather, trust that the time is not right or God has better plans for us and is thus, protecting us from that which is not good for us.

Moreso, as time passes by, we may certainly understand why things happen the way it did for us in the past. For instance, never think that you cannot survive after a broken or one-sided relationship, especially one that gave you more pain than joy, as such emotions come and goes with time, making us stronger. Time the great healer diminishes such heartaches, so just allow yourself the time to heal as *patience is a virtue and you are stronger than you think*. Never resort to alcohol, bad company, evil deeds, drugs or suicide as life is precious and you deserve to be happy. Be resilient, work hard and make wise, good choices, develop a close bond with God, who will stand by you every step of the way throughout the journey of life.

Life is strange and incomprehensible, but regardless of what comes our way, whether laughter or tears, good or bad, never stray from the righteous path. Even in unfavorable or unfortunate situations, God provides support for his devotees. For example, Rama received help from Nishadraj, Kevat, Hanuman, Sugriv and the Apes during his exile. Likewise, Hanuman and Trijata comforted Sita during her times of distress in Lanka, while Valmiki and his disciples were there to support and serve Sita when she was left in the forest.

Therefore, *with every dark night comes the radiant sunrise*, as such, one's distress will not last forever. It will pass with time, the great healer and you will enjoy happiness again. Lift yourself and make the necessary efforts to move forward in life as *"God help those who help themselves"*. Prayer and trust in God that all will be well, as there is nothing in this world that is more powerful than sincere prayer. I can testify to this stance by sharing my personal experience of the most trying time in my life to better emphasize my point about the power of sincere prayer and God's grace.

Aside from the passing of my father, I never knew what grief and distress was until soon after my marriage. In an effort to have kids, I firstly had a miscarriage at 3 months into my pregnancy. Then, after one year my first baby girl was borned prematurely at just 31 weeks. Immediately, she was taken away by the nurse and placed on life support. After an hour, I saw my baby but was not allowed to hold her in my arms. I placed my finger in her tiny hand and she grabbed hold of it while I prayed to the *Universal Mother* to protect my baby. By the next morning, the life support was removed as my baby didn't need it anymore which the doctors stated was a miracle. However, we were told by the doctor that there were some concerns as a result of her premature birth, thus they needed to monitor her closely for the next 3 weeks.

I cried everyday for my baby not knowing what to expect and the fact that she had to stay all alone at the hospital for so many days. While we waited patiently to bring our baby home, we engaged in different forms of worship to God for the health and safety of our baby girl. However, close to the end of the 3rd week, we were told that our baby was diagnosed with hydrocephalous. The doctors needed our permission to have her checked thoroughly by higher experts at the Texas Children's Hospital.

The Neurologist confirmed the diagnosis and informed us that our baby would 'most likely' need to have a 'shunt' done. That is, a tiny tube inserted from her head to her stomach to drain the excess fluid as urine. The doctor warned that if the surgery is not done, the excess fluid will prevent the brain from growing and developing which would result in our daughter being handicap for life. He further stated the 'shunt' is for life and if it becomes clogged during her lifetime, the process would have to be repeated. My heart trembled at the mere thought of my delicate, new born baby having to undergo such a terrible surgery.

Being a very prayerful person all my life, I mentally questioned *'why me'*? My family and friends were very supportive, but I was devastated. We continued with our fasting and sincere worship and that's when I affirmed that *"if the God I worship all my life is real and alive as I believe, then my baby would not have to undergo that dreadful surgery and she would grow and develop normal and healthy"*. Once per week the medical team performed a head scan on my baby to check if her condition was worsening. By God's

Grace, her condition remained 'stable' all along. However, she was not drinking from the bottle, so they continued to feed her through a tube inserted through her nose to her stomach.

Each day seemed like an aeon as my overwhelming distress knew no bounds. Finally, after 2 months my baby was discharged, but yet some unfavorable news. I was told by the doctor that they saw some abnormalties in her brain, so she won't be able to 'walk or talk'. I questioned whether my baby stood any chances of being normal and healthy, but the doctors sadly maintained that they are certain that it will be one or the other – *unable to walk or talk.* I felt absolutely no emotions in my heart as I affirmed mentally that they donot know of the great compassion and power of my God.

Upon taking our baby home, it was the auspicious celebration of Maha Shiv-raatri. At the temple, I offered my sincere worship to *Lord Shiva* praying for my baby to be able to drink her bottle as is normal. The next day my baby pulled out the tube from her nose and we started feeding her with the bottle. By the third day, she was able to drink well from the bottle. I also performed special worship to *Maha Shakti Durga Maata* for the good health of my baby. Two weeks later, two medical therapists from the hospital came to our house to check on my baby to look for vital, normal signs of a healthy baby. My baby completely showed all the necessary vitals indicating a normal, healthy baby. Thus, the therapists left stating that my baby donot need their services.

My baby girl met every timely milestone and is now 9yrs old. She continues to excel in her academic pursuits at school bringing home the 'Honor Roll' frequently. Even from KG level, her teachers were impressed with her brilliant performances. This is the same child that doctors claimed had some abnormality in her brain. If that were true, can she behave normal and excel at school? I don't think the doctor's diagnosis was inaccurate, but the greatest doctor of all is the Supreme Lord. Therefore, our dearly, beloved Lord and Divine Mother heeded our call and made everything right for our baby's health and well-being. Thus, I can testify that God is real, so kind, loving and compassionate.

We may not have the opportunity to see or meet with God in this age/time, but if one is a *genuine seeker*, one can feel God's divine presence within, just like the air that we breathe for survival, but it cannot be seen. It is rightly believed, that when God cannot come, he sends someone as the Lord can adopt any form as he deems fit to answer our call. Thus, someone who comes to our aid in our hour of need is undoubtedly, acting as a messenger of the Lord to bring relief to us like Sri Hanuman.

Life is short, so where is the time to hate, when there is so little time to love, live and enjoy life. So let us not procrastinate, but be kind to fellow human beings as simply putting a smile on someone's face is a virtue, but not at the cost of ridicule to another person. Rather, let us positively contribute to the happiness of others by touching lives while one is alive, *as to what avails sympathy when one has already departed this world.*

Lastly, one must not draw false conclusions or criticize others, *as not everything is always the way it appears to be.* Sometimes, the things that we boast about or despises are the things that life throws at us. Therefore, we must be mindful of how we think, what we say, and the actions we perform, as actions have consequences, *"what we sow is what we will reap"*. If we choose to lead righteous lives, good things may come our way.

Finally, we all have our fair share of challenges in life, so we must not add to the distress of others by being mean and judgmental. Rather, we must focus our energy on our own lives and household, and therefore, respect the privacy of others, as therein lies our best interest and general wellbeing. Afterall, what does it take to be nice to each other and live in peace and harmony with one another in the name of humanity?

In conclusion, I sincerely hope and pray that this brief narration of *Ramayan Katha* provides a better understanding and clarifies some of the misconceptions some may have of our most sacred text, such as (a) Why did Sita crossed the line drawn by Lakshman? (b) Why did Sita take the fire test? and, (c) Why did Rama renounced Sita? I trust that the reader finds this narrative helpful for essential knowledge, as well as enlightenment and self-elevation.